CIARAN CARTY

ROBERT BALLAGH

CIARAN CARTY

ROBERT BALLAGH

First published 1986 by Magill, Merrion Row, Dublin 2.
© Ciaran Carty 1986

Cover design by Robert Ballagh
Printed by Mount Salus Press
Distributed by Eason's
Colour Separations by Litho Studios Ltd.

ISBN 0 907085 70 9

Grant-aided by the
Arts Council

To Julia

ACKNOWLEDGEMENTS

Robert Ballagh's art, life, and surroundings form a unity. This book is a portrait of him in terms of this interaction and would not have been possible without his frank and patient cooperation. My first thanks go to him for responding with such good humour to my incessant questioning and also for making available his extensive photographic files and personal documentation. Unless otherwise stated, all quotations derive from a series of taped interviews held in his studio in May-June 1981, January 1983 and August-September 1985. I have also drawn on material published by me in various publications and catalogues since my first meeting with Ballagh in 1978.

I should like to thank all those close to the artist who gave me so much of their time, in particular his wife Betty, whose forthright comments were always helpful, Micheal Farrell, the late David Hendriks, Kieran Hickey, the late Cecil King, Gordon Lambert, Brian Trench, and, of course, his parents Nancy and Robert. I am grateful to Philip MacDermott for commissioning the book and owe an enormous debt to Vincent Browne and Eileen Pearson for their courage and support in taking it over and ensuring its final publication.

The format of the book is intended, like a Ballagh portrait, to serve as a visual inventory of its subject. This required the advice and expertise of many people. I learned much from Joe Kelly, who was involved in the original production, and I was fortunate in having a fellow art critic, Aidan Dunne, to take charge of the artwork, design and production of the book, and also Pat Pidgeon and David McKenna. Charles Collins, David Davison, John Kellett, Bob Fannin, Randall Faulkner, Tom Collins, John Donal, Kevin Dunne, Ron Mercer, Brian Goulding, Tom Grace, Dave Robinson, the Irish Times, Independent Newspapers, the Sunday Tribune, Magill, the Department of Foreign Affairs, the Arts Council, Brian Trench, the Hulton Press, the Gallery Press, Bjorn Bergvist and the artist's parents all helped with photographic and illustrative material: I should like to thank all of them.

The Publisher would also like to thank the Arts Council for their assistance in the publication of this book.

Robert Ballagh

1

"Name?"

"Robert Ballagh."

"When did you stop working?"

"I haven't stopped working."

The girl behind the counter at the Labour Exchange in Gardiner Street pushes aside the form she has started to fill in.

"You can't make a claim if you haven't stopped working."

"An artist doesn't stop working. He may stop selling and making money. But if he's any sort of an artist, he never stops working."

The girl gives him a withering look. "We have no form for that sort of thing. You'll have to see someone higher up."

Ballagh is received courteously by a senior official at the Department of Social Welfare in O'Connell Bridge House.

"You're not really entitled to claim. But we can appreciate your position. Would you be agreeable to a means test?"

He would.

"Of course, you'll have to promise that as soon as you make a few bob, you'll sign off."

"All I want is survival money for a few weeks."

Embarrassed pause.

"One more thing. I can't sign you on as an artist because no such category exists. Would you mind being an unemployed self-employed labourer?"

He wouldn't.

The following week Robert Ballagh signs on the dole in a queue with itinerants — sherry bottles sticking from their pockets — his fellow unemployed self-employed labourers.

The studio in Parliament Street, within sight of City Hall.
Patrick Collins (inset) once painted there.

9

That was in 1976.

Ballagh had been on the dole before. But not as an artist. He signed on the in 1960s when he lost his job as a draughtsman. There were no problems then.

The implication of this distinction is relevant to any realistic appraisal of the arts in Ireland.

Even at the level of mere subsistence, the artist is popularly assumed to be in some way different to other people.

Everyone has a right to a decent standard of living but there is still a romantic notion that it is the ennobling destiny of the artist to be a genius starving in a garret.

Already in 1976 there was talk of painting and sculpture coming into their own after years of neglect during which Ireland gave a convincing impression of being illiterate in the visual arts.

Ballagh at 33 was internationally respected. The Galerie Isy Brachot in Brussels, the Galerie Liliane Francois in Paris, the Aktionsgalerie in Bern and the N. Treadwell Gallery in London regularly showed his work. His exhibitions at the David Hendriks gallery in Dublin were something of a social event. With his wife Betty he was a guest at Dublin Castle receptions and embassy parties.

Yet nobody thought it incongruous that he had so little to show financially for his success.

Status in contemporary society is invariably measured by material possessions. One expects a top executive or businessman to have a house and car — to say nothing of reserved parking space — to go with their position. But different standards are applied to an artist.

The fact that Ballagh still lives in a simple artisan's cottage in the Broadstone area of Dublin is thought to be quaintly appropriate — as if he were fulfilling an allotted role.

"How lovely to live in the inner city!" people exclaim. "Everyone is doing it nowadays."

The mundane truth is that Ballagh lives where he does because it makes financial sense.

"I'm not being fashionable or campaigning for An Taisce or trying to save wonderful old buildings for the national heritage. I'm just another person who lives there, like my neighbours, because it's economically viable."

Attitudes to "art" and "the artist" are coloured by the distorted associations which accrue to the actual words. Mass media communication reduces experience to headline simplicities — the all-embracing label — which become more real to the public than the reality they are supposed to signify. Issues are trivialised as slogans: PRO-LIFE, ANTI-NUCLEAR, WOMEN'S LIB, BRITS OUT. Everyone is tagged from birth according to colour, creed and nationality — a depersonalising process by now so habitual that it is taken for granted.

In this context the typecasting of "the artist" as someone unconcerned by the everyday — a genius transcending his time and creating art purely for art's sake — is accepted unquestioningly even by artists themselves.

Robert Ballagh is one of the few not to conform: both the content and the form of his painting are a demystification of art and the artist.

"Artists are of their time and the art they make is conditioned by the time they live in," he says.

"They're fooling themselves and everyone else if they fuss about at the edge of society saying — 'I'm pure, I'm a virgin, I won't sully my hands.'

"It's like being a passive smoker. You're taking it in anyway. To imagine the artist to be untouched is all a huge illusion.

"I think artists should jump in at the deep end and experience everything. The more you experience, the richer your work will be. If you're going to deal honestly with your own circumstance, you must be part of it. You can't be on the outside looking in."

There has never been anything immaculate about the conception of art. The very notion that there ought to be is itself socially conditioned by developments peculiar to the last century. The emergence of a dealer-gallery system, in place of earlier traditions of direct patronage, for a while pushed artists into the position of being outsiders, alienated from any integrated role in society.

Art is inevitably the work of a particular person in a particular place at a particular time. As such it is shaped by social and political realities ("the complex construction of a number of real historical factors," Janet Wolff argues in her book, *The Social Production of Art*).

Art is as much a part of the social framework as any other process of production. There is nothing ethereal about the artist. He does a job like anyone else. The significance of an art work is no more a purely aesthetic matter than the Olympic Games or Ireland touring South Africa in rugby are purely to do with sport. Everything that happens in society — whether art or sport or religion — is conditioned by the evolving interaction of the historical, economic and personal elements that make up that society.

Our appreciation of Renaissance art is dependent on the knowledge that it is in fact a product of the Renaissance. Art simulating the same style today would be rightly disregarded as junk.

The primitive cave drawings in Altamira in Spain are notable precisely because they are the first manifestation of art in the Ice Age 14,000 years ago.

Even the so-called purely formal "art-for-art's sake" abstraction of a Newman or Rothko means little except in relation to Modernism in New York in the mid-twentieth century.

No work of art can ever be completely self-contained, no matter how rigorously it might aspire or pretend to be. It is of necessity located in and affected by social circumstances.

This is the general truth underlying Karl Marx's dictum that "it is not the consciousness of men that determines their being, but, on the contrary, their social being that determines their consciousness."

Which is why Ballagh doesn't feel any of the conventional qualms about accepting commissions. The snobbery that it is in some way a less pure form of art — a kind of selling out — stems from a failure to recognise the social origin of all art.

"I love the idea of art being used and if it's commissioned, it's always going to be used. Somehow or other it makes an artist feel like an attached person. It defines your role as an artistic tradesman to the bourgeoisie. It prevents you over-emphasising the role of the artist as being desperately significant."

The printed circuit board normally hidden away inside computers has become the medium for a revolutionary new art form he pioneered in 1986 with James Barry and James Malone of Circuit Arts. By bonding copper on to the board and coating it with an ultra-violet light sensitive photopolymer they were able to create images which were then screenprinted in limited editions for the American and Japanese computer market.

There's no need to go anywhere as culturally refined as a gallery or a museum — the new churches of a twentieth century that has made a religion of art — to come in contact with his images.

Post a letter and the stamp you lick may well be one of his — he's designed special issues every year since 1972.

Students dining in the UCD cafeteria in Belfield enjoy the colour and light of huge sliding screens which he created according to Leger's concept of art being for the people.

Multimillion deals at the Fitzwilton headquarters were until recently conducted amid the abstract *ambiance* of his murals of shapes and colours that look like maps but mysteriously don't refer to any known geography.

Shoppers queueing with their trollies for the checkout at the 5-Star supermarket in Clonmel appear to mingle with his life-size figures of people looking at paintings ranged along the way.

His art, in keeping with that of someone who started out as a pop musician, is all about making contact with the public.

"The visual arts are a means of communication and if you want to communicate, surely you want to communicate with as many people as possible. You use a language that is universally accessible."

To him designing posters for the Dublin Theatre Festival and the Irish Ballet Company, a set for Barry McGovern's one-man Beckett show *I'll Go On,* book covers for the Poolbeg Press, credit titles for Kieran Hickey's movie *The Light of Other Days,* illustrations for Paul Muldoon's poems or even a mural celebrating the achievements of the ESB are all equally valid forms of art.

"Nobody thought less of Goya because his work was for patrons.

"If you see your role as doing a job like anyone else, you know where you stand, you do your work and occasionally you may not only solve the simple problem of the commission — painting the subject well — but maybe, like the great artists of the past, you will transcend all this and make some contribution to art that outlives the present.

"Certainly for me this is how great art can be made: an artist, working on simple problems of the present, through his own skill and experience makes a picture that not only deals with the reality of the present but reaches beyond it."

3

Not troubled by scruples about aesthetic purity that inhibit more conventionally trained artists — he derived most of his art education from the Ritz cinema and the *Eagle* comic — his approach to technique is as open as his choice of themes.

He'll use any process that works to produce an image and avail of any mechanism to disseminate that image — realising that it's the image that matters and not how it has been produced.

Photographs culled from magazines were originally the source of many of his images. When he couldn't find the ready-made shots to suit his purpose, he acquired a second-hand Rollei camera and began taking his own.

People don't sit for his portraits. Instead he photographs them from different angles, recording their every expression and gesture and the details of the environment with which they choose to surround themselves. He doesn't capture the soul so much as offer a visual inventory of the subject's life.

He has been able to keep comfortably clear of the dole since 1976 by painting portraits — notably Noel Browne, Hugh Leonard, Bernadette Greevy, James Plunkett, Brendan Smith and Charles Haughey — and in so doing developed a language which led into more autobiographical and self-questioning works which point to a new direction for painting in the 1980s. Not that he would admit to any distinction between commissioned work and his "own" work.

"It would be unwise to invest any one form with more significance than another. Perhaps in years to come my stamps will be considered more important than my painting!

"But I agree that there are areas you can't get at in commissioned work, that you can only tease out by following your own way."

Following his own way has caused him to break with the Modernism he espoused in his early days as Ireland's first Pop artist and "to re-connect" (as he puts it) with the older traditions of Western art.

The stunning achievements of Impressionism, Expressionism, Fauvism, Dadaism, Cubism and Surrealism generated in the later twentieth century the false expectation that art must always be a Giant Leap Forward for Mankind. Tradition became a dirty word. The cult of the "Briefly New" dictated that each new "ism" automatically invalidated all that had gone before. Styles proliferated like haute couture fashions and were almost as ephemeral.

More recently Pop Art, Op Art, Kinetic Art, Post-Painterly Abstraction, Minimal Art, Conceptualism, Performance Art and

Environmental Art — to mention a few — in quick succession jostled for supremacy with various critics as the One True Way.

Clement Greenberg, one of the high priests of Modernism, as recently as 1980 at the AICA conference in Dublin decreed that art could have nothing to do with anything other than itself: it was purely about form.

Ballagh's attitudes outside art — particularly his socialist involvements — made it unlikely that he would simply indulge in an art that didn't say anything.

As early as 1969 his paintings were beginning to make statements although still packaged in the Modernist idiom.

Pop Art blandly accepts mass media reality as it is. But Ballagh's series of split images of marchers, burning monks in Vietnam, refugees and firing squads in South America — for which he was chosen to represent Ireland at the Paris Biennale — were a direct expression of the concerned consciousness of the 1960s.

He won the Alice Berger Hammerschlag Award in 1971 with brash contemporary copies of Goya's *Third of May,* Delacroix's *Liberty at the Barricades* and David's *Rape of the Sabines* – images that apart from being stylish pastiches could be read as a plea for tolerance in the North's internecine conflict.

Ballagh intuitively anticipated the Post-Modernist retreat from formalism which by the 1980s was to hold sway particularly in architecture, the most visible of all the arts and therefore the first to signify change.

The message from new buildings in America is no more glass boxes. Tower block jungles are in disgrace. Dogmatic functionalism has given way to an awareness of architecture as language. Tradition has been rediscovered not in the form of imitation but as quotation.

"For the artist, creating the new means choosing the old or the existing," announced Robert Venturi. Philip Johnson, whose glass and pink granite ATT building in Manhattan has become a symbol of the movement, proclaimed: "You cannot not know history."

This revisionism — a going forward by looking back — became apparent in Ballagh's painting in 1975 of the *Tristram Shandy* commission, inspired by the Laurence Sterne novel and based on direct literary quotation, the ultimate apostasy of a Modernist cult that insists on referring to nothing other than itself.

But the direction he was to take had even earlier been hinted at in the New Realist series of people looking at paintings — ironically the springboard for his international reputation — in which he parodied the contemporary mode of thinking of art in brand image terms.

This turning point was also reached by his close friend Micheal Farrell, who gave him his start as a painter in 1967 when he hired him to help with two murals for the National Bank.

The purely formal range of hard-edge abstraction proved too limiting to contain Farrell's feelings. Looking to older French painters such as Daubigny and Boucher, he found the stimulus for a more personal and human style.

"It depends on your way of thinking," Farrell told me. "I feel that my vocabulary is much wider now than it was before. I can put humour into my work. I can put in different aspects of my character and personality rather than make it just an art work."

Modernism's obsession with originality for the sake of originality never had much affinity with an Irish consciousness steeped in the past and in literary expression. "Few of us have the grace of prophecy or the ability to make a new and ennobling popular image," the sculptor Oisin Kelly used say. "To re-set and sharpen an old one that has become worn is excitement enough."

But Ballagh stands out as the first avowedly Modernist painter in Ireland to make a self-conscious and systematic attempt to rediscover the past, updating a traditional language of perspective and literary allusion to give expression to recognisably contemporary concerns.

This is the real significance of the quotations from Vermeer in *The Conversation* and Velazquez in *Winter in Ronda*: he is reasserting the fundamentals of Western art in the light of all that has been learned from modern art.

"Art cannot escape the past and the traditions that are ingrained in our consciousness. We have to see where we come from. We have to recognise that we go back further than the Modernist experience.

"Just to date your awareness back to Cubism is to give yourself a very small spectrum to work from. If you have a broader base behind you, the range in front of you will be broader too. The trouble with Modernism is that it has become too narrow, particularly for the public.

"You can't divorce form and content. Reality is a soup: everything is mixed in there. We see and we think and we read and you can't compartmentalise these different functions and say that a person *only* sees or *only* conceptualises.

"A painting must have something to communicate. This is the springboard it jumps off from, what I as an artist put into it. But the form it takes is a vehicle which will affect the communication and if the form is not adequate, the communication fails and the work fails."

The film-maker Jean-Luc Godard once likened this relationship to the human body: the skeleton and the flesh. "To me," he said, "style is just the outside of content, and content the inside of style, like the outside and inside of the human body — both go together, they cannot be separated." The analogy appeals to Ballagh (many of his influences are rooted in cinema). "One cannot survive without the other. To separate them is to murder the artwork."

4

The whole elitist notion of "art" being by the few for the few — an exercise in form without reference to time and place — has nurtured the phenomenal growth of the international art market in the twentieth century: there is a vested interest in its continued currency.

Some indication of the scale of this market is the fact that Sothebys and Christies alone netted over £350,000,000 auctioning art in 1979.

Ten Impressionist paintings sold for £22.9 million in Sothebys in 1982, with the Degas pastel *L'Attente* going for £2,337,500. By 1986 Christies in New York would have been disappointed not to knock down 20 million dollars in a single night's sale.

The lack of apparent content in abstract art in particular ensures that its value can be more readily subjected to the rules of pure economics and finance — like oil or gold or any other commodity.

It has by now become one of the safest of all investments — hoarded in vaults as a hedge against inflation — precisely because each art object is unique and unvariable. The fact that there is only one of it is assiduously cultivated because scarcity determines value under the laws of supply and demand.

But the quality and power of an image — as distinct from the market potential of the object in which it is embodied — is in no way dependent on it being a one-off, handmade, original object.

Walter Benjamin, whose essay *The Work of Art in the Age of Mechanical Reproduction* has long interested Ballagh, pointed out that from a photographic negative one can make any number of prints: consequently to ask for the "authentic" one is to make no sense. The moment that this criterion of authenticity in art breaks down, the entire function of art is transformed. The way is open for painting to become — as it has for Warhol and Ballagh — the production of an art work which has been designed to be reproduced. The artist can reach beyond the narrow audience of the gallery-dealer-critic system and reach a mass public.

This readiness to harness art to technological advances has a natural affinity with Ballagh's long-held socialist conviction that art belongs to everyone, not just a cultural aristocracy. He has no sympathy for an art of esoteric indulgence.

"I don't make images that are complex and difficult to come to grips with. My pictures look a certain way because I use a visual language that has had a common currency since the Renaissance.

"Even a child can understand perspective. After 500 years looking at it, nobody is perturbed that a building shrinks on the canvas. But before Giotto people wouldn't have understood this."

Ballagh's unabashed willingness to utilise the mass media to communicate the content of his art and make his images known to a public outside the immediate art world has left him open to accusations of "commercialism". His work has sometimes been denigrated as "merely illustrative" and "painting to numbers".

Yet the fact is that all western art is ultimately commercial. It is made to be bought and sold. It feeds off the capitalist market system or a system of State support (through which the *avant garde* are tending to become *de facto* as secure as civil servants). To pretend otherwise is a self-delusion to which all too many artists blithely succumb.

As Che Guevara wrote, in an essay heavily underlined by Ballagh: "If the rules of the game are respected, all honours are obtained — the honours that might be granted to a pirouetting monkey. The condition is not attempting to escape from the invisible cage."

Perhaps independence for an artist lies in making the "cage" visible: in seeing it for what it is.

5

The conditions in which art happens — why it happens where it does when it does — are determined by a rich interaction of complex social, historical and personal factors.

It wasn't some accident of birth that Vermeer and Rembrandt

emerged in Holland in the seventeenth century and that over a period of fifty years many of the greatest painters in western civilisation all lived in a tiny country smaller than Ireland. Their flowering was a logical consequence of the growth of a hugely successful trade empire which established an affluent merchant class with the will and the inclination to patronise art on a grand scale.

"I believe that talents falls fairly evenly throughout the world but that it flourishes where conditions are ripe," says Ballagh. "Like in a garden when you put down seeds: if the ground is fertile, they'll grow better."

Ballagh himself — and the whole new generation of artists to follow him through the 1960s and 1970s — is a vivid embodiment of this process of conditions improving to make art possible.

During the 1960s Ireland was jerked abruptly into the twentieth century, revolutionised by a sustained pressure of enormous economic and social change.

The momentum of successive Programmes of Economic Development pioneered by Lemass and T.K. Whitaker, the introduction of national television and the airing of taboo issues on popular programmes like Gay Byrne's *Late Late Show,* the impact of the Second Vatican Council and the spread of free secondary education for all — these factors were to combine to transform what had been a predominantly agricultural, isolated, conservative, Church-ridden rural economy into an industrialised fully paid-up member of the European consumer society.

Skyscraper office blocks were already beginning to overshadow Dublin's sedate Georgian squares by the late 1960s. Suburban housewives drove to work in second cars while foreign *au pairs* minded their babies (and the babies of the affluent new middle classes were fewer as the Pill became as commonplace as Valium tablets). Office girls jetted to the Austrian Tyrol for winter sports holidays. De Valera's vision of an Irish Ireland rooted in the honest truth of the soil and rural dignity of Gaelic culture seemed as distant as the Celtic twilight.

In ten years from 1958-68, industrial output surged upwards at an annual rate of 6.4 per cent and industrial exports jumped from £26 million to £146 million. Over £250 million in capital funds flowed in to the Republic as 350 new foreign-owned companies were lured by bountiful tax concessions to set up business there.

Irish products became household words on the world market. The

British grew fat on Irish butter. Scandinavians furnished their houses with Tinatawn carpet. Italians munched Jacob's cream crackers. Americans tucked into Irish beef and Gaelic coffee. Spaniards found Guinness good for them. Aer Lingus achieved the highest load factor of airlines on the North Atlantic route.

Industry by then accounted for 30 per cent of the national product, agriculture for only 20 per cent. With over one million people the Dublin area had become the most populous part of the country as workers quit the fields not for the emigration boats but for city factories and offices. More marriages and earlier marriages combined to create the youngest population in Europe, with nearly fifty per cent under 25 years of age.

"One cannot radically change the material culture and hope to preserve the rest intact," Father E.F. O'Doherty pointed out in *The Furrow* in 1962.

The corollary to Ireland becoming a dynamic and youthful urban economy has been a fundamental change in cultural attitudes and in the role of arts in society. With prosperity came more enlightened patronage both by the State and by the burgeoning middle classes.

In 1949 Professor Thomas Bodkin's *Report on the Arts in Ireland* had protested gloomily that "no country in Western Europe cared less, or gave less, for the cultivation of the arts."

But whereas Dublin had only one commercial art gallery at one stage in the 1950s, it now has as many galleries as cinemas. Banks and insurance companies have built up major collections of contemporary Irish art. No self-respecting middle-class home is complete without original art works by living Irish artists. Every annual show of the RHA is replete with portraits of the new technocratic and entrepreneurial ascendancy. The Arts Council has become a source of livelihood and encouragement for emerging young artists (and through Aosdána for older ones who have fallen on difficult times).

Traditionally artists in Ireland tended to come almost exclusively from one stratum of society — the Protestant Anglo-Irish minority with its roots in the privilege of the Pale and the Big House (it was this, rather than any lack of male chauvinism, that explained the preponderance of women painters in the early twentieth century).

The opening up of Irish society and the widening scope of the Arts Council under Colm Ó Briain in the 1970s generated a climate in which artistic expression could become accessible to all the population.

Ballagh belongs to a new breed of artists who have been enabled by these changes to function as artists in Ireland. Before the 1960s even Jack B. Yeats found it difficult to sell paintings in Dublin. The economic base simply wasn't there, nor the willingness of the Church and the State to support art.

"But now there is a market here for art. The artist can work within his own environment and speak to his own people. This is a good situation to have going."

Not that there has been anything automatic about the process by which this came about. A complicated interplay of social elements may influence who becomes an artist and the kind of artist they become. It may influence the form and content of the art produced and how it is received and evaluated by the public and by history.

But each and every art work is ultimately the result of individual choices by individual artists. It happens as a consequence of an individual response to experience. It is not a preordained reaction to fixed and determinate stimuli.

"Your art comes not just from being yourself, but through pre-conditioning you've experienced over the years," says Ballagh.

That is its paradox: like life itself it is both predetermined and free. Not to recognise this essential duality — to maintain that art is *solely* the throw of a loaded dice or *solely* a flash of individual genius — is to deprive it of the magic that makes it what it is.

This book will attempt to unravel the intricate interplay of social and personal elements that have come to make Robert Ballagh the kind of artist he is.

It is not a conventional biography as such. Nor is it an academic critical assessment. It certainly does not conform to the conventional concept of an "art book".

My hope is to uncover — through the particular experience of a particular painter in a particular place at a particular time — some of the ways in which art can happen.

Since art *is* a social artefact — a product of its time and place — it follows that all art is inherently regional.

"Internationalism in art enabled the artist to escape from dealing with the situation in his own region," Ballagh complains. "I agree with Picasso that there are times when it becomes dishonest for the artist to remain silent.

"The artist has a responsibility to the present time."

This raises the whole question of the Irishness of art — not as a sentimental label but as an inherent part of the social reality which conditions it.

The sense in which a painting is "Irish" or — "politically committed" or "Catholic" or whatever — is something innate in the conditioned sensibility of the artist rather than imposed arbitrarily like a thatched cottage in a landscape or Celtic ornamentation in a hard-edge abstraction.

Art is a litmus paper of its time. It is a two-way mirror of experience.

This book is a look in that two-way mirror.

This photograph, taken in 1979, is the source for the self-portrait in *No. 53, Winter in Ronda*

23

1

"I had an impulse from an early age to take the opposite view to the established position on anything. I suppose I've always been a natural dissident"

1

His studio is high above Parliament Street, looking out on City Hall. The Olympia Theatre and Project Arts Centre are around the corner. You can smell the Liffey when the skylight is open.

It's up several flights of lino-covered stairs. Security alarms glow red. Intimidating signs say: GUARD DOG BEWARE!

"Nothing to do with me," he says reassuringly. "Who'd want to steal paintings. It just happens that lots of businesses have their offices in the building."

It's always been an artist's studio — one of the few in Dublin with any continuing tradition. This is where George Campbell and David Hone once painted. Arthur Armstrong too. Patrick Collins would throw parties — and guests went home with sore heads from the low ceiling on the landing if not from the booze.

There is a sense of history about the place. A decomposed body was found under the floorboards years after the Civil War. Brendan Behan and Cathal Goulding stayed here for a while in the 1950s.

Almost a pastiche of the popular idea of the artist's garret where genius awaits the flash of inspiration.

But Ballagh has no time for that.

"It's simply a place to work. Like any other office."

He paints from nine to five every weekday, commuting across the city by bicycle from his home at Temple Cottages in the Broadstone.

The work in progress in the summer of 1981 is a portrait of Desmond Downes, of the bakery family, with his wife Margaret, a leading accountant, and their children Rachel, Lucy and Alexander.

The start of a portrait. Photographs of the Downes home overlooking the Liffey Valley, gummed together to suggest possible backdrops for the eventual grouping of figures.

The canvas is set up directly beneath a high window in the ceiling which fills the study with dusty sunlight. The air is oppressive. Like a glasshouse.

"I once surrounded myself with a polythene structure — like an oxygen tent — to prevent dirt getting on the paint and on the glazes.

"That's one of the difficulties working in old city buildings. Particularly on a windy day when the panes start rattling. There's so much dust in the air.

"I was also able to lay paper on the roof of the polythene and so diffuse the light. Canvas is a textured surface and with the sun shining directly down, all you'd see — even with the very fine cotton duck I use — would be the weave of the cotton, the bumps and hollows of the surface rather than what you were actually painting."

A background of wooded hills with a river winding through them is shown in minute detail in the portrait: almost every leaf would stand up under a magnifying glass. But the figures of the Downes family, grouped on a tiled patio of a restored stone schoolhouse overlooking the Liffey valley, are only blank outlines at this stage.

"It's a perverse way to work, I suppose. Doing everything else first before starting on what is, after all, the whole point of the portrait: the subjects whose likenesses will decide its success or otherwise. You're playing Russian roulette. You've put in too much work to turn back. You're committed to the result. You've got to get it right."

"I find this is a way of ensuring tension. When you're working over a long time, there's a danger that your concentration and attention will flag. If you do the figures first, you might be tempted to rush off the background."

This is his first real landscape of any kind — but it is far removed from the traditional Irish idyll of a Paul Henry or a Sean Keating. Quite clearly it is going to project an image of city people in the country. What we see is a view that they have bought for their pleasure: it is evidence of their affluence.

The portrait is a quotation within a quotation. It is modelled on Gainsborough's *Mr & Mrs Andrews*. But by implication it refers to the Marxist critic John Berger's celebrated analysis of that famous 18th century portrait as an example of art as a social statement.

Obviously neither Gainsborough's nor Ballagh's paintings can be regarded in purely aesthetic terms: each in its different way makes manifest the social standing of its subjects (with the ironic historical distinction that Mr & Mrs Downes merely own the view, whereas Mr & Mrs Andrews obviously owned the actual landscape as well).

"You can overdo the sociological analysis, of course. But to deny it is folly. You need to place a painting in the context of the artist's career and of human history in order to understand it properly. An artist and his art are prisoners of their time."

As Ballagh is of his. It's no coincidence that he paints the country with a city feel. That is the Irish reality of his experience.

"It's not that I don't like the country. But I'm a city person by nature and by conditioning. For me to attempt any other imagery would be dishonest, a denial of my own experience.

"I think there are very few people now who have had any kind of rural experience of the kind propagated for so long in art and which reflected de Valera's naive belief that Ireland somehow could be kept in the 19th century in terms of culture and ideology." De Valera gave voice to this in a celebrated Patrick's Day broadcast on Radio Eireann in 1943:

That Ireland which we dreamed of would be the home of a people who valued material wealth only as a basis of right living, of a people who were satisfied with frugal comfort and devoted their leisure to the things of the spirit; a land whose countryside would be bright with cosy homesteads, whose fields and villages would be joyous with the sounds of industry, the romping of sturdy children, the contests of athletic youths, the laughter of comely maidens; whose firesides would be the forums of the wisdom of serene old age.

That same year the Irish Exhibition of Living Art was launched by Mainie Jellett, Norah McGuinness, Louis le Brocquy and others who wanted to open Ireland to the stimulus of the Modernist ideas that were revolutionising international art and to challenge the academic stodginess and stage-Irish sentimentality of the Royal Hibernian Academy.

Robert Ballagh too was born in 1943.

His art was to derive its tension from the tug-of-war between these two conflicting visions of Irish culture.

2

Art and violence are part of the same process in Ireland, like the positive and negative in photography.

"I think it's because you have two tribal cultures colliding," the poet Michael Longley once told me. "On one level the sparks that fly are street violence, riots and murder, but on another more imaginative level the sparks become artistic expression."

Another Northern poet W.R. Rodgers talked of "the creative wave of self-consciousness" which occurs when two racial patterns meet.

It can hardly be a coincidence that the most violent decade the North has known should also have been its most culturally creative. Seamus Heaney, Derek Mahon, Longley himself, John Hewitt, Paul Muldoon and a whole new generation of younger poets have made a contribution to literature far out of proportion to the size of the tiny corner of Ireland from which they come.

"The confluence and confusion of different tones and colours is enriching," says Longley, referring to his own Protestant upbringing and the Catholic tradition with which he was later to become involved.

"One is obliged in terms of friendship, let alone in terms of art, to attempt to define and redefine oneself and one's attitudes. That's bound to bring a kind of alertness that will give edge to the paintings, the plays and the poems."

There are differences of emphasis in time and place in the responses to this fusion of cultures.

The North, with its own unique historical and constitutional evolution, is perhaps nearer to the stage the South reached at the turn of the century. It is going through a political and cultural ferment similar to the literary renaissance of Yeats and Synge and the Abbey Theatre but also to the blood sacrifice of 1916 and the internecine divisions of the Troubles and the Civil War.

The volcano is active there: in the South it has grown benign. But the reverberations are still stirring. They condition the ambiguous reaction to the H-block protest and the hunger-strike deaths. They give tension to the art.

Robert Ballagh embodies this cultural division. It is in his blood and upbringing. His father's ancestors were Ulster Presbyterian, his mother's Southern Catholic. But as always in Ireland the labels are deceptive. They imply extremes in attitudes that the reality of his background belies.

The name Ballagh in fact comes from the Gaelic war cry *Fág an Ballagh,* which means "clear the way" (the "h" being an aspiration of the "g" in Gaelic). The family goes back to the early Christian centuries and Niall of the Nine Hostages: it was one of the Ulster tribes. Somewhere along the line, many of the Ballaghs became Presbyterians.

Recently, Ballagh has re-established contact with relatives and namesakes in the district of Castleshane, County Monaghan, where his grand-uncle ran a thriving flax and saw mill. But the name is still common enough for there to be another Ballagh with whom he has been confused in vaguely sinister circumstances.

Special Branch detectives called on his father one night apparently looking for this Ballagh.

"You're too old," they said, disappointed. "Have you a son?"

Warned by a call from his father after they left, he rang his friend and solicitor, John Gore-Grimes, who is prominent in the Irish Association for Civil Liberties. "He read me my rights as an Irish citizen but finished by suggesting that, if they were operating under the Offences Against the State Act, I would be well advised to cover my balls."

He waited that night for the knock on the door that never came. Later he learned that he shared the same surname with a young Republican.

The lineage on his mother's side is no less diffused and contradictory. Her father was a Bennett from Limerick, her mother a Smithwick from Kilkenny. The Bennetts were rural Catholics, but well-to-do. They employed labourers on their farms. An uncle was a Cumann na nGaedheal TD in the 1930s. Ned Murphy, a former *Sunday Independent* political correspondent, recalls George Westrop Bennett as a gregarious companion.

"We used go swimming together. A gentleman all the way. But Castle Catholic."

Not the family to be too put-out by a daughter marrying a Protestant. Nevertheless Ballagh's father converted to Catholicism, part of the easy-going tolerance that was to make a success of the marriage.

"Robert's father was a sportsman with all the integrity one associates with sport," remembers Gordon Lambert, who used play tennis with him at the Mount Temple Club.

"Nancy his mother was always stylish and very elegant.

"I can see a combination of the two parents in every painting Robert paints.

"They gave him a tremendously stable background."

But the Ballaghs were middle-class without the means to go with it. Few had in Dublin during the 1940s. There was a burgeoning white-collar population but the economy was still under-developed and predominantly agricultural. Consumer society affluence was yet to come.

They lived at 14 Elgin Road in Ballsbridge: a good address even if it was only a flat. It was as comfortable as they could afford living off the salary his father earned marketing shirts for Ferrier Pollock.

There was a faded elegance about the broad tree-lined avenues and rows of tall Victorian houses, each with their landscaped gardens and flights of stone steps leading to columned doorways: the echo of a colonial past.

The post boxes with their royal insignia had been painted over in patriotic green. Gaelic equivalents (which few residents could pronounce) had been found for street names that read like a roll call of imperial glory: Waterloo, Prince of Wales, Wellington, Clyde and Churchill.

The suburb was developed in the 19th century to provide the families of army officers and civil servants — the ruling ascendancy — with a fashionable environment similar to that to which they were accustomed in England.

It was convenient to several schools — Masonic, St. Andrews, Wesley, the High School, Alexandra — modelled loosely on English public school principles. There were churches to serve the spiritual needs of every Protestant persuasion from High Anglican to Seventh Day Adventists. The Royal Dublin Society, provided cultural outlets with its library and recital rooms and a fashionable occasion to rival Ascot with its annual Horse Show. Lansdowne Road was the home of Irish rugby, nearby Londonbridge road the headquarters of hockey, and in the summer there were half a dozen cricket grounds within walking distance, to say nothing of the bowling greens at Herbert Park and Railway Union.

With the establishment of the Free State in 1921, one privileged group merely replaced another: if anything the area became even more exclusive. So much so that eminent medical men, Government ministers, civil servants, university professors and High Court judges were to react with some indignation in the 1950s to a suggestion by American Congressman John J. Rooney that the new American Embassy at the corner of Elgin Road was being sited

Nancy and Robert Ballagh outside the flat at 14 Elgin Road,
Ballsbridge.

in "a slum neighbourhood".

The *Irish Times* quoted a resident as saying that the fact that some of the houses had been let in flats did not mean that the area was "going down". It was still "most desirable" for professional purposes.

3

Robert Ballagh was born on September 22, 1943, an only child. "But I never regarded myself as an only child. There were two boys in the upstairs flat and a girl and two boys in the next door flat. It was like growing up in the middle of a community — all in the one house."

The date makes him a Virgo, a person destined by the stars to have artistic leanings. But he regards astrology as mere superstition. "I never read horoscopes. It's a matter of chance when someone is born. There's nothing ordained about it. A slip on the stairs during pregnancy could accelerate the moment.

"We thought our daughter Rachel might be born on my birthday in 1968. But she was two days later. Which makes her a Libra with a radically different birth sign to mine. That doesn't make sense.

"If any date is important it should be when you're conceived rather than when you're born."

That's a belief he shares with Tristram Shandy, a frivolous delay in whose conception, according to novelist Laurence Sterne, fundamentally altered his future personality and predestined him to a life of misfortune.

> Pray, my Dear, quoth my mother, have you not forgot to wind up the clock?
> —Good G—! cried my father, making an exclamation, but taking care to moderate his voice at the same time — did ever woman since the creation of the world interrupt a man with such a silly question?

The novel *Tristram Shandy* – probably the first in English to break away from conventional plot and chronology and deal with the nature of fiction itself — was later to become a crucial influence in the development of Ballagh's art. Particularly with its idea of chance as being in some paradoxical way predetermined: you had to be in the right place at the right time to take advantage of it.

Images of protest, Silhouetted marchers, symbolising 1960s political concerns, one of the *Series 4* paintings in his first one-man show in 1969. Acrylic on canvas panels, 72 x 72.

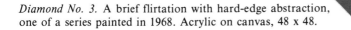

Diamond No. 3. A brief flirtation with hard-edge abstraction, one of a series painted in 1968. Acrylic on canvas, 48 x 48.

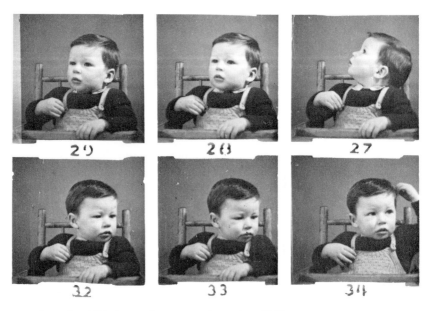

2 5   2 6   2 7

3 2   3 3   3 4

An only child. A set of contact prints, circa 1945.

Unlike the wretched Shandy, "begot and born to misfortune", Ballagh was to mature in an Ireland of the 1960s uniquely suited to his talents. Nothing to do with the stars: simply the logical consequence of radical changes in the social framework.

There was little about his childhood to suggest that his future might lie in art. This in itself is significant. The conventional idea of an artist — then, as now — had nothing in common with the kind of artist he was to become. The mould out of which he came anticipated this difference.

Ballsbridge for much of the 1940s was almost without traffic. He remembers the first car after the war. The family couldn't afford one until he was in his teens. The occasional open-deck tram rattled along the Merrion Road. Every morning he awoke to the clip-clop of the horse-drawn bread van from the nearby Johnston Mooney & O'Brien bakery. A dog could sleep in the middle of Elgin Road without being disturbed except perhaps by a football. "We were able to stretch a string across from two lamp-posts as a net for tennis!"

It wasn't like growing up in a city and yet it wasn't the country either — except on days the farmers came up for the Spring Show or the bloodstock sales at the RDS. His parents didn't have to worry about where he played. He was free to roam off on adventures with his gangs of friends. The only time he was in trouble was if he came home dirty. His mother was a stickler for cleanliness.

From an early age he developed a sense of gregarious independence. He'd go fishing for sprats along the banks of the River Dodder. Herbert Park became a jungle of the imagination with its exotic shrubs and chestnut trees: sometimes in winter the duck pond froze and was great for skating. The surrounding gardens with broken glass on the walls were secret places to explore, orchards to rob on night raids.

Every Saturday he'd queue with his pals for the fourpenny rush at the Ritz cinema — popularly known as the Shack — which was on Serpentine Avenue.

"We thought the end of the world had come when the price went up to eightpence.

"I saw every Saturday and Sunday matinee and if I was lucky my parents would take me at night during the week. There was nearly always a double-bill in those days so I must have seen at least six pictures a week throughout my childhood."

The week's programme was advertised on a billboard in Ballsbridge.

"Everything had to be hand-painted. I remember I'd watch for hours the man doing the hand-lettering, fascinated by his sheer skill. I thought the layout was fabulous although it probably wasn't. But at least it was neat and tidy. That impressed me.

"Hand-lettered signs are coming back again, now that perspex is so expensive. I still stop and watch. It's a joy that's never left me. Particularly if there's a bit of gold leaf. That kind of skill is wonderful to see."

All this was before Cinemascope. The screen hadn't yet widened out into a letterbox. The cinematic images he saw up to the time of his Confirmation, when he was taken to *The Robe* as a treat, were in the old square academy ratio.

Cinema was the dominant cultural influence of his childhood: reality perceived in terms of photographic images. The experience offered glimpses of worlds excitingly different to his own. America became like a real place to him. He walked Fifth Avenue in his imagination, looked out over Central Park from a skyscraper apartment, cruised Sunset Strip in a Cadillac.

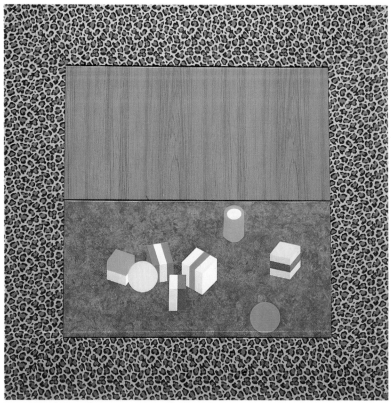

Kitsch in a fine-art setting. Dolly mixture sweets framed with velvet. Acrylic on canvas, 56 x 56.

Third of May, after Goya. His earlier treatment of a Spanish painting, restating a familiar masterpiece in a contemporary political context. Acrylic on canvas, 72 x 96.

People and a Matisse, a 1975 work in his people looking at pictures series. Acrylic and oil on canvas, 51 x 32.

Two Men and a Roy Lichtenstein, acrylic on canvas, 96 x 96.

Movies were to shape his way of seeing as a painter. Photo-realism became his natural idiom of expression, pop images his vocabulary. Subconsciously, he even painted many of his early works according to the format of the academy scale of the screen on which he saw his first pictures.

He went to kindergarten at Miss Meredith's, a private girls' school in a Georgian house at the counter of Pembroke Road. It then had a reputation for encouraging children to have a mind of their own while valuing the social graces. Pupils were taught to walk straight by balancing books on their heads. There were dancing classes for 6-year-olds in which the girls sat on one side of the room and the boys had to walk across and ask for the pleasure of a dance.

Not that he needed much encouragement to be sociable. He was forever in the thick of things, always with some scheme afoot. Like putting on puppet shows for the neighbourhood, charging thruppence admittance (which invariably had to be returned: he'd get into an argument with his associate and the stage would topple over).

"It was the making of the thing that really appealed to me. I loved putting together the puppets and painting the sets. The actual performance didn't interest me so much."

He also made model airplanes. "You'd spend months working on it but the chances were it would crash into a wall at the first go. So you'd delay flying it. Particularly because the wretched diesel engine always cut your fingers. But you daren't admit that."

He was taken out a lot at night by his parents — one of the advantages of being an only child — and became familiar with a grown-up world his pals hardly knew. He remembers being brought to ballroom dancing classes run by his aunt Evelyn Burchill, who was the doyenne of the profession and had a studio over the Stella Cinema in Rathmines.

"I'd be left sitting in the window, watching the queues forming below for the double bill. The music was going slow-slow quick-quick-slow. I couldn't understand why people had to go through such a rigid discipline simply to enjoy themselves."

There were outings to Butlin's holiday camp at Mosney to watch Evelyn's husband George demonstrate the tango with his partner Madge. "The two figures were caught in the spotlight going round and round. It looked like a movie. Finished like one too. They ran off together!"

Childhood holidays on his great-aunt's farm at Patrickswell.

All his mother's family lived on the land around Limerick. As a small boy he would go on holidays to his great-aunt's farm at Patrickswell.

"One of the labourers, Billy MacNamara, would take me under his wing. The family wouldn't see me all the time I was there. I'd go everywhere with him. Feed the calves. Draw the water from the well. I could see that it wasn't an easy life. They had to get up at five and work eighteen hours a day to live. My great-aunt had a big farm and was relatively well-off. But even she had no running water. Electricity was just for lights. The loo was outside. The radio had to be run off wet batteries. Yet this was a life-style De Valera was extolling at the time as an idyll for the nation. People living on the land never saw it that way. They wanted something better. They voted against it with their feet, emigrating in their hundreds of thousands throughout my childhood."

4

He was now going to St Michael's, a preparatory school for Blackrock College. But getting a private education marked him off from most of his friends, who went to the national school at Haddington Road.

"They'd jeeringly call me a Protestant snob whenever we had a

Joseph Sheridan Le Fanu. The image is a play on the writer's concept of horror as something in the reader's mind. A window opens on his interior world and on his death dream of a falling house. Oil and acrylic on canvas, 60 x 48.

Portrait of Bernadette Greevy. A continuous loop tape of Greevy singing Brahms is triggered by the viewer's presence. Oil on canvas, 48 x 48.

row. Somehow privilege then was identified with being a Protestant. Not that I considered myself privileged. I suppose we were lower middle-class. My father was something of an armchair socialist and always referred to himself jokingly as a counter-jumper. But education defined class in those days."

Blackrock College had been established in 1860 by the French Holy Ghost Fathers to meet the need for Catholic secondary schooling following Catholic Emancipation. Catholic schools, being precluded from public funding of any sort on the grounds that they were denominational, lagged behind the so-called non-denominational Protestant-controlled schools. No public status or recognition was given to their courses of study. Professor Mahaffy of Trinity College could jeer that the new Catholic schools were "institutions calculated to produce saints perhaps but not scholars."

Blackrock, known originally as the French College, set out to show that given the same opportunities, Catholic students could compete as equals in the State exams. It fielded rugby teams that began beating the ruling elite at their own game. Among its pupils were Eamonn de Valera and Cardinal Dalton. The future Archbishop of Dublin John Charles McQuaid had been its Dean of Studies and President in the 1920s and 1930s. It had helped shape the new Catholic Ireland. This was its cherished tradition.

But in the 1950s homilies about being privileged to take on the role as "leaders of the nation" didn't impress youngsters like Robert Ballagh. "I found it offensive to be continually reminded that we were an elite. I didn't consider myself better or worse than anyone else. Many of my friends were working-class. One was the son of a bus conductor. Another had a father working at Johnston Mooneys."

Hardly a day passed without a visit to the Dean of Discipline to get the strap. He was in trouble not for failure at studies but for breaches in conduct and deportment. One week he was blacklisted for eating chips on a bus. He was expelled for a day for talking to a girl from Sion Hill at a rugby match. He refused to raise his hand at Confirmation to pledge that he would abstain from alcohol.

"I had an impulse from an early age to take the opposite view to the established position on anything. I suppose I've always been a natural dissident."

His father was summoned to the college, but he always took his son's side. As a convert he took a more liberal view of education. He had none of the inherited Catholic awe of a priest. He believed that children should be encouraged to think for themselves rather than to conform all the time to the established way of doing things.

Both of them were disappointed at his failure to make the rugby team: they used go together to the rugby internationals at Lansdowne Road.

"I was much too small. The guys on the Junior Cup team were 12 to 15 stone. I was only about 6 stone. I got murdered whenever I

Shortsighted and too small, but *(front left)* he made the St Michael's rugby team in 1953-54.

played. It was an act of mercy I wasn't picked."

To add to his difficulties, he was short-sighted. He could only field a high ball by guesswork. "I'd run around in circles and someone would yell — 'A little to the left, a little to the right!' "

He didn't begin wearing glasses until he was 16. He was up in the gods at the Olympia Theatre watching *The Scatterin'* with a friend, who remarked on the expression on one of the actor's faces.

"But you can't possibly see any faces from up here," he exclaimed.

"Of course you can. Try my glasses."

Only then did he realise that he had been half-blind all his childhood.

This may relate to his inability to work with numbers. Mental arithmetic has always been beyond him. He can only do a sum — even simple addition of double-figure numbers — by writing it down on paper and visualising it.

"I always have to accept change on trust or ask someone to check it for me!"

Drinking fountain at Ringsend. From his book of Dublin photographs.

Portrait of Hugh Leonard. The playwright is shown at his desk as if in a still from one of the old Hollywood movies to which he's addicted. Oil on canvas, 48 x 60.

The Conversation. Ballagh reconnects with Vermeer. An ironic homage to the Dutch master's *Artist in His Studio.* Acrylic and oil on canvas, 72 x 96.

Favourite reading. The *Eagle* comic with Frank Bellamy's Dan Dare strip and the centre spread with the flat finish that conditioned the look of Ballagh's later art.

All his reading as a boy tended to be visual too. He devoured comics, never missing an issue of the *Eagle* with its stylish art work, and Frank Bellamy's wonderful drawings in the Dan Dare comic strip. There was always an airbrushed drawing of an aeroplane or a ship across the centre spread: years later the same flat finish was to show in his paintings. He collected Marvel and DC Comics, attracted by their American feel and their sense of fantasy: they reinforced the cultural conditioning he was getting from movies.

Later he went with his father to the RDS Library, where he invariably took out picture books. He discovered that by far the most profusely illustrated books dealt with art. By the time he left school he was familiar with the imagery of all the great masters. He could even imitate his favourites.

About the only classes he enjoyed at Blackrock were those given in art by John Coyle, a figurative painter of considerable ability who exhibited regularly at the Royal Hibernian Academy.

Art occupied a lowly place on the curriculum — a subject for those not clever enough to do anything else — but Coyle managed to instil a sense of its possibilities. "Remember that Picasso mastered all the basics before he defied them," he used tell his class.

"He would divide us into those who could and those who couldn't draw a straight line. I was always among the former. For that I'm grateful to him. He even persuaded the priests to permit slide lectures on the history of art. But the nudes had to have tape stuck over their breasts and genitalia!"

Around that time Ballagh conceived the idea of making a totally original art object that would flabbergast the world.

"It seemed to me that art had never succeeded in portraying movement. With my passion for making things, I constructed from soldered tin a little man in running motion, which I called The Rapid Man, and I then welded on little spikes which I called arcs of motion. The thing looked like those multiple image photographs of a golfer's swing."

But a week later he flicked open an art book at the RDS to be confronted by the very same idea. Not only that — but by an artist with virtually the same name. It was futurist Giacomo Balla's famous painting *Dog on a Leash*, showing a dog with its legs in a whirl of motion.

Early pop. He was 16 when he drew this self-portrait, which anticipates his realist style.

EIRE 8

EIRE 17

éire BSL 1927-1977 ESB 10

EIRE 15

AN CHÉAD GHLAOCH TELEFÓIN 1876

EIRE 5

UPU 1874-1974

EIRE 7

UPU 1874-1974

EIRE 30

COMMISSIONERS OF IRISH LIGHTS

EIRE 9

AN CHÉAD GHLAOCH TELEFÓIN 1876

EIRE 3½

AN tEAGRAS MEITÉIREOLAÍOCHTA DOMHANDA

EIRE 12

AN tEAGRAS MEITÉIREOLAÍOCHTA DOMHANDA

EIRE 10

FIRST EAST-WEST TRANSATLANTIC FLIGHT 1928

29

EIRE

Boys' Brigade 1883-1983

EIRE 22

AN BLIAIN CHUMARSÁIDE DOMHANDA

EIRE 29

AN BLIAIN CHUMARSÁIDE DOMHANDA

EIRE 22

Seán Mac Diarmada 1883-1916

EIRE 19

AN ÓIGE 1931-1981

EIRE 46

Aer Lingus 1936-1986

PÁDRAIG Mac PIARAIS 1879-1916

eire

"It was a very early lesson for me. The quest for originality is a stony road."

Not that he had any thought then of ever becoming an artist.

His father brought him to carnivals and rugby matches but also to the Living Art and the RHA exhibitions.

"I remember doing pastiches of Louis le Brocquy which my mother showed proudly to friends."

He still has a self-portrait he did at school when he was 16 that anticipates elements in his present realist style.

But painting was never more than something he did on a rainy day or when he was sick. His dream was to be a pop musician.

Rock'n'roll was sweeping Ireland. He identified with its rebellious city feel, its flouting of convention, its rhythm and blues energy. All his pocket-money went on 78s of the new tunes which, to learn the words, he played over and over again on an old-style gramophone — the kind that had to be wound up and had venetian blind shutters for volume control.

"I knew every song recorded by anyone. I could even tell who sang the backing vocals. My knowledge was encyclopaedic."

He was electrified when he heard Bill Haley's "Rock Around the Clock" over the titles of the movie *Blackboard Jungle,* which he saw with his father at the Carlton. He saw the movie *Rock Around the Clock* thirteen times. He got a guitar and formed a group with his pals, Paul Hennessy on rhythm guitar and Alan Devlin on drums,

A selection of commemorative postage stamps designed by Ballagh. From top left: Scouting in Ireland 1977, Scouting in Ireland 1977, Electricity Supply Board 1977, The First Telephone Transmission 1976, Universal Postal Union 1974, Universal Postal Union 1974, Commissioner of Irish Lights 1986, The First Telephone Transmission 1976, World Meteorological Organisation 1973, World Meteorological Organisation 1973, The First East-West Transatlantic Flight 1978, Boys Brigade 1983, World Communications Year 1983, World Communications Year 1983, Sean MacDiarmada 1983, An Oige, Irish Youth Hostelling 1981, Aer Lingus 1936-86 1986, Padraig Pearse 1979.

Liberating music. An *Evening Herald* advertisement for Bill Haley's *Rock Around the Clock,* which he saw thirteen times.

later replaced by Paul Loughlin. Devlin went on to achieve notoriety in 1985 as the actor who walked offstage in the middle of a performance of *HMS Pinafore* at the Gaiety.

Even before he left school they were playing semi-pro at tennis club hops.

"I was a fair to average lead guitarist. But there was very little spontaneity in my playing. I learned everything off by heart note by note — and it was note by note perfect."

One night he tried dum-di-dumming on the lower strings instead of playing the lead passages — and realised that that was really the way he preferred his music. He felt a natural empathy for the bass. It was always the part he heard in any music he listened to.

"Electric bass guitar probably appealed to me because it was a completely modern instrument. It hadn't existed before. You couldn't even buy one at first. I made my own by sticking pick-ups onto an ordinary guitar.

"It's not a solo instrument and yet a group can't really exist without one. It's fundamental to the whole sound. A good bass can make a group, a bad one ruin it."

He'd sit in with Paul at music lessons with Bob Phillips, a professional dance-band man later crippled as a result of a motor cycle accident.

Through Phillips he got his first gig with professional musicians. Chick Smith, a trumpeter who had been in the big time in England until his lip started going, needed a guitarist to make up the numbers for an engagement his touring dance-band had booked in Galway.

The band picked him up in their van at the Four Provinces. He had to walk into town in the snow. The drive to Salthill took all day. The band had flasks of whiskey and rugs to keep out the cold. They left the boy to shiver in his wet clothes.

"Nobody had told me to bring a dress suit. They could only find me a jacket at the ballroom. So I had to stand behind the amp for the whole gig, in order to hide my wet shoes and trousers.

"But the funny thing was that I was the only one in the whole outfit who knew any of the new tunes. They were completely out of touch, a dance-band still in the swing era. I had to play *Guitar Boogie Shuffle* fifteen times during the night to keep the punters happy."

The drive back to Dublin was a nightmare. A draught from a slit in the van door cut through him as he huddled in his damp clothes. It was early morning before he got to bed. He stayed there for a week with 'flu. His fee was £7.

Not the recommended way to study for the Leaving Certificate. But school by then had become almost an afterthought. He was lucky to get two honours in the exam. Far from brilliant but sufficient to secure a place at Bolton Street Technical College studying architecture.

John Coyle had told him before leaving school: "I'm not saying you should take up art, all I'm saying is that you could. You have the talent. And if you ever decide to take it up, don't let anything stop you."

But his parents ruled out any such idea from the start. Even Jack Yeats hadn't been able to sell paintings at a recent show in Dublin. Picasso prints had no takers at the Ritchie Hendriks gallery at a mere £25 each. Art was no kind of a career for their only child.

Perhaps they were influenced too by the tragic suicide of his cousin Noah, a son of the actress Ruth Durley, who had been showing considerable promise as a painter. Not that his death had anything to do with art. He had been upset over losing a girl. But they were adamant that they didn't want another artist in the family.

Still less a pop musician: that was not the future they had in mind for a boy with his education. He realised he would have to try what they wanted before he could go his own way.

But architecture should not be seen as a second choice and merely something he was forced to do.

"Once I got into it I thoroughly enjoyed myself. It began to seem for a while like what I had always been destined to do."

A classmate remembers him as a brilliant sketcher. "He was always first with the 'in' word. But not all aspects of architecture appealed to him. He once arrived at a building construction exam, took one look at the paper and walked out!"

Robin Walker was back from the United States full of enthusiasm for the Modernist style. He had worked with le Corbusier in France and Mies van der Rohe in Chicago.

"It was like Moses coming back from the Mount. We were getting pretty much the message first hand. His lectures were enormously exciting."

Walker laid emphasis on a practical approach to problem solving. You didn't just take a blank sheet of paper and start designing. There had to be a logic and a reason behind everything you did — the principle came first. Essentially the Bauhaus line: form follows function.

"It's very much under attack now. But while some of the applications can be criticised, the principle is correct. It still guides me."

He had always been attracted to the clean look of things. The neatness of the hand-painted movie advertisements. The tidy finish of his model aeroplanes.

"I'm not a person for the primitive gesture. The precise way of doing things has been a constant in my life. It is much easier to dash something off. But my nature has never let me do that."

Bolton Street was in a sense like a college of art for him. What he learned there was to resurface in his painting.

All his work is designed according to scaled architectural plans. Everything is calculated and worked out, with tracing paper and T-square on a drawing board with Miesian precision. Where lines cross, they cross in the right place. No awkward things happen.

The rules of perspective that had been inculcated in him did not immediately influence his painting: the pop images of his early period were strictly two-dimensional. But later in the 1970s, when he rejected the dogmatic formalism of Modernism to reconnect with the older tradition of Western art — the whole Renaissance picture-making process of perspective and illusion — he was also reconnecting with his student training as an architect.

At this time he got into the habit of going on sketching outings with a friend Michael O'Sullivan in a second-hand Morris he had bought with money earned playing gigs. They would drive up to the Featherbeds in the Dublin Mountains or to White Rock on the Vico Road, Killiney where he used to swim as a boy, drawing places they liked rather than the well-known landmarks. Sketches of Booterstown station and the White Cottage show him toying with a style that was slightly arty and less precise than any of his architectural drawings.

By then he was in his third year at Bolton Street. He was doing stints in architects' offices to get practical experience. He began to realise that it might be years before he ever got a chance to design anything significant of his own.

All the energies of the profession seemed to be concentrated on creating more office space. Yet Dublin had an appalling housing shortage. Every week the homeless were out on the streets in protest marches organised by the Dublin Housing Action Committee.

"I was becoming involved in a profession that was totally cynical about all that. Architects wouldn't admit that they had a social role.

Drawing places he knew. A student sketch of Booterstown railway station.

They claimed that a building was a building, that they were purely concerned with aesthetics. But that was a delusion. Their reality in fact was cash.

"We can see now the consequences of their failure to grasp the nettle in the 1960s. The greed of the speculator has ravaged Dublin. But when I was a student the first speculative office blocks hadn't yet been completed. A choice could have been made."

5

He led a double life during these years: attending lectures by day and playing gigs at night. He bought a bass guitar and auditioned for a semi-professional showband called the Wolverines. It split up before he could play a gig. But a few of the members then became the Concords.

"We played anything and everything. Most of the lads were 'fed heads' — that is, union musicians, members of the Federation of Musicians. They could play the newspaper if it was put in front of them. They followed no fixed programme. It depended on where we were and what the punters wanted. If old-time went down well, we'd play it all night. Somewhere else, it might be Latin American type tunes. The only music they couldn't crack out was pop. That's where I came in with Liam Hurley, a brother of the popular singer Red Hurley. Our role was to keep the young city crowds happy. It was a musical education for me."

The Beatles were taking off. There was a resurgence of rock'n'roll. It was the right time to meet up again with Alan Donaldson. They had strummed their first guitars together. Now he called himself Alan Dee and was the lead singer with the Chessmen. He needed someone to replace their bass, who had gone sick.

Ballagh required little persuasion. The Chessman were all his own age. Their music was his music. It was the music of the moment.

The seven-piece group, managed with flair by 20-year-old Noel Pearson, even then showing the drive and audacity that were to make him one of Ireland's most innovative theatrical impresarios, were already on their way up the charts. Alan wrote the songs and played electric organ. Willie Halpin, now a teacher at the College of Music, played guitar, John O'Sullivan played baritone sax and Terry Brady was drummer, with Pascal Haverty on tenor sax. Davey Martin, who had played with the Radio Eireann Symphony

Moving away from architecture. An impression of Misery Lane, made while still at Bolton Street Technical College.

Orchestra, introduced a classical tightness to the brass. All the English bands at the time were just guitar groups, but the Irish showbands had brass: this was their distinctive contribution to pop music.

Teenyboppers swooned at their gigs. Pearson papered the big working-class suburbs of Walkinstown, Finglas and Ballymun with pin-up photographs. A girl in Crumlin started a fan club. Clearly it was time to go fully professional and play the whole country.

He was disillusioned with architecture. Probably his heart had never really been in it. But the decision finally to quit was made for him. He played a country gig while sitting for his third year exams, got back at 9 the next morning and fell asleep in the middle of a paper. Permission was refused for him to repeat in autumn: he'd either have to sit for all the subjects again or stay on for an extra year. He opted instead for a career with the Chessmen.

The Irish showbands, which provided the only live entertainment in rural Ireland, were among the highest-paid in showbusiness. Having grown out of the dance-bands, they were totally unionised. Nobody could be paid less than the Federated Union of Musicians rate. There were standard minimum meals for out-of-town engagements.

Over 600 registered bands were then playing ballrooms up and

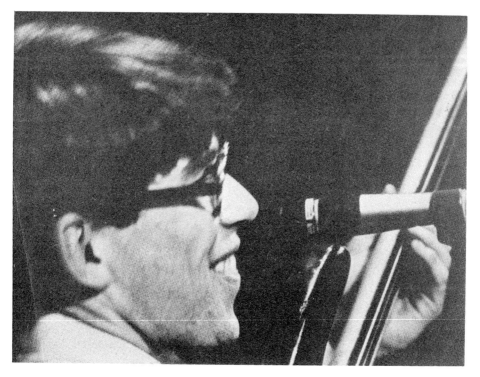

Teenybopper pin-up. Playing bass-guitar with the Chessmen in the '60s.

down the country. Now in the 1980s there are fewer than 100.

The money was way ahead of Britain. Once when the Chessmen were playing in an Irish club in Manchester, Ballagh looked in on the Cavern in Liverpool where the Beatles had started. He got talking with the singer from a group playing there.

"What's the money like?"

"Ten pounds."

"That's very little."

"Well that's the standard fee you pay to play here."

"You mean *you* pay?"

"But of course."

That same night the Chessmen were getting £250.

They were particularly popular among the Irish emigrants. They'd play to 5,000 a night at Cricklewood or Hammersmith. But it

Moving up the charts. With the Concords and the Chessmen.
His union card. The Chessmen fan club membership form.

was a saddening experience. They could tell the year someone had left Ireland by the tune requested. The GAA results were read out at the break. Most of these people would spend the rest of their lives in England but they hadn't integrated with the English. They were an abandoned generation, the human reality behind the shibboleths of de Valera's Irish Ireland.

Playing both Protestant and Catholic halls in the North every weekend provided a chilling intimation of the violence and hatred that were soon to rend the country apart.

"Do we play the Queen?" he inquired once in Dungiven, unsure of the religious geography.

"You play the Queen and you'll be shot."

The band was not going down well that night. His informant took him aside. "You've got to give them the ballads." So they played rebel songs into the early hours. Afterwards they got drinking. Much of the talk was about guns in the attic.

"We're ready for the Prods," they were told.

A Protestant girl who followed the band around the country, told him in Belfast that she'd have to miss the next gig there.

"Why?"

"You're playing in a Catholic hall."

He was earning more money than he had time to spend. He drove a flashy Ford Corsair. He ate in expensive restaurants. He wore exclusively tailored suits. On a whim he'd fly over to London just to see a movie. £100 a week was like £1,000 in today's money.

He was still only 21.

There were recording sessions at Ardmore Film Studios, interrupted on one occasion by Richard Burton, who wanted to see rushes of *The Spy Who Came In From The Cold.* Pearson fixed them up with their own sponsored radio show *The Chessmen Half-Hour.* They made the Top Ten with a song by Alan, inspired by what they'd seen in the emigrants' clubs in England, called *Michael Murphy's Boy:*

> *I can't get a decent job*
> *To bring me in a few bob.*
> *I'm just one of a mob*
> *An' filled with discontent.*
> *The bit I've had's been spent,*
> *Or lost, or drunk or lent.*
>
> *But I won't go, I won't go,*
> *I'll give it one more try.*
> *My name is Patrick Joseph –*
> *I'm Michael Murphy's boy.*

They built up a repertoire of over 100 tunes, keeping up-to-date by learning two or three new ones every week. They'd sing up to 60 a night on out-of-town gigs. In Dublin they could be more selective; a young group called the Black Eagles, with Phil Lynott as lead singer, played warm-up for the first half of their dances.

They never saw half the places they played, arriving after dark and leaving before dawn. It was better than staying over. That left too much time to fill in and nothing to do but drink. He enjoyed the camaraderie of being on the road. But there were tensions too. Not because the band didn't get on with each other but simply out of exhaustion of being all the time together.

"I could tell by then that I hadn't the makings of a true musician. I was very competent at what I was doing. But I hadn't any potential to build on.

"It's okay to make rock 'n 'roll when you're young. But when you're 60 you're not going to be able to get by doing the same. If you're going to give your life to music you have to be able to grow into other forms of music. I'd a pretty shrewd idea that I didn't have anything like that in me."

They had started out playing progressive rock 'n 'roll out of sheer pleasure. They'd weave the brass into a tapestry of sound, using it as ornamentation like James Brown, the negro singer who played at the Apollo in Harlem. Other Irish bands tended to keep it separate, blasting out the melody in unison with the trumpet on top.

The Ritz cinema, later the Oscar Theatre. Sometimes he saw six movies a week. With comics, they provided his early art conditioning.

But in three years their programme had been stood on its head. Nobody outside Dublin wanted to hear rock 'n' roll orchestrations of classical music like the William Tell Overture, which was the kind of music the band liked to make. More and more they found themselves dishing out monotonous country and western hits.

"We could play it as well or as bad as leading C'n'W stars like Larry Cunningham. But we played it professionally, without conviction; whereas they *lived* it. Their sincerity and our lack of it shot across. We were just city slickers trying to pull the wool over their eyes."

Ballagh invariably did the announcing. One night he realised that he hadn't called a single tune he liked during the whole gig.

"The joy had gone out of my music. Once a realisation like that sets in, every time you play becomes an agony."

It was time to get out.

He contacted Phil Lynott, who was then playing bass with a group called Skid Row.

"Like to buy my guitar?"

"Sure."

He never played again.

With Micheal Farrell in 1981 in front of one of the murals for the National Bank which led him into art in 1967.

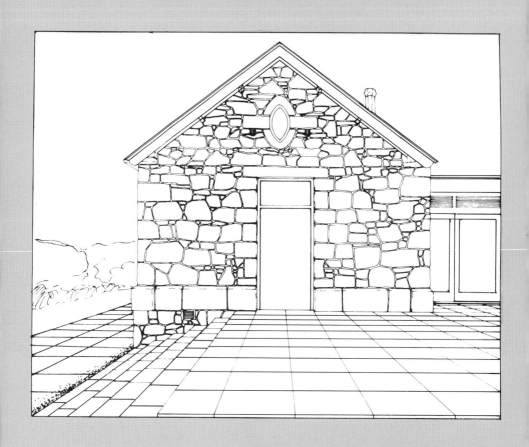

2

"I don't think you can make art without some stability. You have to have a fixed place to make it. You can't be living from one bedsit to another."

1

Tags of masking tape are sticking to his fingers as he lets me in. He has been using it to cover over areas of the completed landscape and the outline of the figures in the Downes portrait. The idea is to isolate the patio so that the tiles can be painted with a roller without letting the paint seep over the rest of the canvas.

"Using a roller is a way to avoid artificial artistic patterns building up when you have to deal with a large flat area of paint."

That had happened with the stonework.

"I dabbed the colour on with a sponge and found I was subconsciously creating effects. But somehow it suited the stone."

It would be all wrong for the tiles. The roller will keep the application of colour automatic in spite of himself.

"What I like about it is that you don't have aesthetic control over how it happens."

The trick is in the mixing of the paints. The ground colour is applied wet. He uses an alkyd liquid resin which is quick-drying. He mixes the colours a little early so that they become slightly tacky. He puts the darker colour on a sheet of glass, then runs the roller over its surface — always using an old roller — and applies it on top of the ground colour with a quick movement of the wrist. The result simulates the manufactured look of a real tile.

He'll paint the tweed jacket on Desmond Downes in the same manner — but using more colours rather than simply a dark against a light tone of the same colour. Purple, brown and black will be overlaid to convey the woven texture of the material.

The architectural approach. A scaled front elevation drawing of the Downes' home, derived from the earlier photographs.

"When you overlay colours, the roller picks up the earlier colour and transfers it on and adds the darker one so that you get a pattern that is constant throughout and fairly close to tweed.

"When it goes right, it looks outrageously simple to do. In a couple of seconds you have it. But it's hit or miss. You either get it right or you don't. If you don't get it right, you have to wash it off and start all over again."

Which can be expensive. Each time he fails he wastes £5 to £10 worth of paint.

"I find it a good idea at times to have someone at my side to help out. Like a surgeon being able to call for a scalpel or forceps. Because it all has to be done so very quickly and in one go."

He has argued for a return to the old tradition of the master painters who thought nothing of allowing apprentices to complete whole passages of their paintings.

"If someone can do a job as well as you yourself can, let them do it. In the heel of the hunt, what's finished and what you're left with — whether it's a photograph or a painting or a drawing — that's what matters. The process is not important except to the degree that it conditions the result. To say that some approaches are invalid and others are not is ridiculous. It's the end result that counts."

Putting this principle into practice under modern conditions can be complicated. Campbell Bruce from the National College of Art, taking him up on an article he wrote on the subject, persuaded him to use two students as apprentices for a portrait of Sheridan Le Fanu which the Arts Council commissioned in 1976.

"It took a lot of nerve to allow them to cooperate at every stage of the painting. They were handy with their hands and good learners. Eventually it worked out well. But it's so difficult to co-ordinate everything when you're working with other people. You have to spend so much time working out who's going to do what. In fact the picture took much longer to paint than if I'd worked alone.

"The trouble is that for all my belief in the principle of delegation, I'm not very good at it. I get too nervous. Particularly if there's something I've spent a long time working on. It worries me that the other person may not understand or be appreciative of what I'm trying to do."

Betty, his wife, is almost the only person with whom he can work comfortably. She helped by painting large areas in the paintings *Winter in Ronda* and *Inside No. 3*.

Modern art is prejudiced against the idea of apprenticeship. This has to do with the way art is regarded in society. It is seen not as a cooperative activity but as the gesture of a loner.

"There's this attitude that if I allow others to paint part of my pictures, then somehow they will not be as good as if I did them all myself. It carries connotations of cheating.

"Yet it's the only way to inculcate what the reality of being an artist is. If you take an artist into the College of Art to teach he's completely out of his proper environment. He's not working there as an artist but as a teacher. The roles are completely different.

"But if the student works with the artist in his studio, he's not simply learning how to apply paint and all the other tricks of the trade. He's learning almost by osmosis the reality of being an artist. Because the artist will talk with him about the day to day reality of it all. He'll pass on the *attitudes* of being a painter."

That is how Ballagh himself became a painter. Through working with another painter.

This was the only art training he ever received.

2

The interview, if it could be called that, took place in Toner's pub in Merrion Row. As did much that happened in the Dublin art scene in the 1960s.

"Can you draw a straight line?" Micheal Farrell asked.

"I think so."

"I'll pay you two quid a day and all the drink you can take."

"You're on."

Farrell was back from New York preaching the gospel of hard-edge abstraction that then dominated international art. He had been commissioned to paint two huge acrylic murals for the National Bank in Suffolk Street. He needed someone to mix paints and help out generally.

"I didn't need to have any experience as long as I had two arms and two legs!"

The work was done at Ardmore Film Studios — the only place big enough for the canvasses.

"They were about 30 feet high and 60 feet long. We needed scaffolding to get up at them. It was like painting a film set."

For Ballagh it was a crash course in contemporary painting. The murals were a hard-edge abstract treatment of vaguely Celtic shapes — linking triangles and circles. Acrylics had been used before in Ireland in the conventional way, squeezing out the paint and applying it with a palette knife. But Farrell sprayed it on. This was a new technique. It posed a whole new set of problems.

"There was a lot of blending and shading involved," Farrell recalls. "But the paint kept drying off before we could achieve the proper gradation of colour. If you sprayed too much it would run. If you didn't spray at all, it would dry up. We must have used 20 miles of masking tape trying to get it right."

They had to work virtually non-stop, 12 to 18 hours a day, completing the two canvasses in five weeks.

"Bobby was terrific," Farrell remembers. "He picked things up very quick. There was a great efficiency and thoroughness about him."

So much so that Ballagh finished up more or less painting the triangle mural while Farrell painted the circles.

"The experience was short-lived but it inculcated in me a sense of being an artist. Before I went into it I still had no idea what I wanted to do. When I came out I more or less knew."

He'd always imagined painters as being remote from the life he knew — names under the reproductions in the books he borrowed from the RDS. Farrell brought painting down to earth for him. He was somebody he could talk with. He led a life like anyone else.

They'd drink afterwards in the bar at Ardmore. Peter O'Toole was filming *The Country Dance.* They became friendly with him and were eventually offered jobs as scene painters. Farrell took up the opportunity. He got a union card and moved to Pinewood, becoming an expert in matte shots — a very difficult technique which involves painting on glass and then shooting through it. He was to create some of the Transylvanian landscapes in the Hammer horror movies of the 1960s.

Ballagh stayed behind in Ireland. For the first time in his life he felt inhibited by a sense of responsibility. He wanted to marry and settle down.

He had met Betty at a beat club two years before. She was sixteen and had already left school. She was working at the New York Dry Cleaners where her father had been manager before his death.

Beat clubs with fluorescent lighting and high decibel canned music were the half-way stage towards today's disco era. Popular

A touch of the Left Bank. With Betty, Tim Goulding and other friends at Toners pub in the 1960s.

music had gone stereo. The 78 era was over. Technological innovations were revolutionising the record industry. Manipulative big business elements were taking over. He was well out of it.

There was a period of uncertainty after he quit the Chessmen. He did nothing for several months. He had worked almost without a break since leaving school. He missed out on all the things students normally do. He never hitch-hiked around Europe or earned pocket money canning peas in the summer holidays. He needed time to get his bearings.

"Meeting Betty was probably the best thing that could have happened to me at that time. I'm the sort of person who could have codded around. I could have been doing this and that for years."

He considered going back to Bolton Street to finish architecture. He lived for a while in a bedsit in Earls Court and bluffed his way into an architect's job by pretending to have left his diplomas at home in Ireland. Betty persuaded him to come back to Dublin. He

67

took a job as a draughtsman with George Milners, a company which was supplying most of the aluminium windows and curtain walling for the new office blocks going up all round the city.

The pay was good. The Draughtsmen and Allied Technicians Association (DATA) negotiated a deal with management which guaranteed an automatic increase every year. But within three months he was out on strike in a dispute over staffing. Being articulate he found himself co-opted on to the office committee. He negotiated with the Federated Union of Employers. He took part in talks in the Labour Court. He appeared in the High Court after Milners were granted an interim injunction against picketting.

"We won in the end. The court order was quashed. The dismissed workers were reinstated. But it was a pyhrric victory. On our first day back we found that a time clock had been installed. This was ridiculous. Draughtsmen don't work regular hours. They have to be on tap whenever architects or builders have a problem. You can't expect them to clock in like office clerks. I could see the way things were going. So I got out."

Noel Pearson had branched into the rag trade. He ran the Betty Whelan model agency. He needed brochures and catalogues in a hurry. Ballagh designed them for him. Pearson was in the record business too. There were labels and sleeves to design. One job led to another. He found he could make a living from freelance design. He updated the logo for Galtee cheese. His father gave him work designing brand tags for shirts. The Wheelchair Association of Ireland needed flags for their annual collection.

During a lull in commissions he went on the dole. In the queue at Gardiner Street Labour Exchange he met his friends from Milners. They had been made redundant.

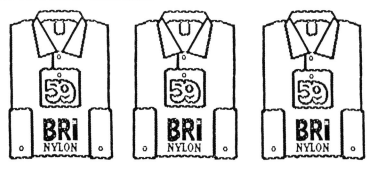

Freelance design. Brand tags for Bri Nylon shirts, which helped pay the bills when he quit the Chessmen.

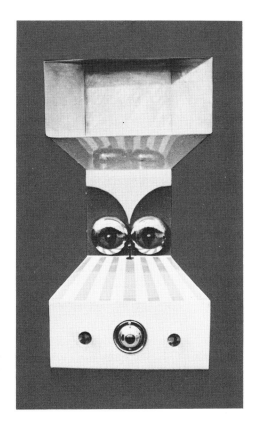

Debut as an artist. His pinball construction, one of the first Irish pop art works, shown at the 1967 Exhibition of Living Art. 24 x 18. Since destroyed.

He was drifting into art. His experience of architecture had impressed on him the need to understand the nature of a problem before trying to solve it. He had a facility for doing pastiches of paintings he liked. But he didn't know anything about what happened in a painting. He knew what he liked but not why he liked it. He didn't know how a painting worked. It was no surprise when the Irish Exhibition of Living Art in 1966 rejected one of his first attempts.

He decided to stick to what he knew. The only art experience he had was in making things. He had made puppets, model aeroplanes, even an electric guitar. Now he tried his hand at three-dimensional objects. Using aluminium sprayed with cellulose, he constructed a small pinball machine that rang a bell when a button was pushed. It was only 24 inches by 18 inches, as was another piece, in which he assembled pieces of aluminium to suggest an erotic torso.

They were accepted by the Living Art the following year and created a stir as the first Irish pop images. But surprisingly, bearing in mind the American orientation of his childhood, they owed more to the English trend of folkloric and heraldic pop than the American preoccupation with consumer items. They looked more like fairground things than something off the assembly line in Detroit. In making them he had half in mind remembered associations of the carnivals he used go to with his father.

Working with Micheal Farrell that spring gave him the courage to paint. With hard-edge abstraction and the experience of using acrylics he had acquired the beginnings of a language.

"The difficulty was to find a way of applying it to the kind of things I wanted to do and say."

There was trouble with his parents. It seemed to them that he was becoming a drifter. He had no steady job. They were understandably worried.

"I remember going to talk to them about it," Micheal Farrell says. "I agreed with them that art was a risky profession. But I assured them that Bobby would be all right. That he was going to be a very good painter. That they should have no worries."

3

It was psychologically the right time to become an artist. Betty had become a steadying influence in his life.

"I don't think you can make art without some stability. You have to have a fixed place to make it. You can't be living from one bedsit to another."

Betty was a third generation Dubliner like himself — although her surname Carabini was even less Irish-sounding than his own. Her great-grandfather had been Italian but her mother was an Ormonde and she had grown up in the Broadstone area.

Her mother, although she moved to Manchester since becoming a widow, had kept up the tenancy at No. 3 Temple Cottages. Although Betty was superstitious about going back to live where she had grown up, they decided to make this their home.

The marriage was at Haddington Road Church on July 1, 1967. Farrell was best man, the only one of his friends who had a suit, and Paula Rockett was bridesmaid. The exotic list of names on the register was not untypical of Dublin's rich cultural mix.

The acceptance of his two constructions for the Living Art came as a timely wedding gift. It was like getting a union card as an artist. He had a sense of belonging. Even better, he was singled out for praise by most of the critics.

"The first moment of contact with this year's Living Art was promising," announced the *Evening Press.* "Robert Ballagh's Torso (£84) attracts with its two aluminium bowls with blue-painted buttons suggesting eyes and breasts . . . "

Dorothy Walker hoped in *Hibernia* that she would see more of his work, which she praised for being "remarkably vigorous and making statements with a strong feeling for shapes which is all-important in three-dimensional work of this kind."

He was automatically invited to the opening of Rosc, the first of a series of international shows organised by Michael Scott which have since proved to be a seminal influence on Ireland's cultural evolution.

"Overnight I seemed to have entrée everywhere. I was rubbing shoulders with artists like Barnett Newman. I felt a part of the whole art world."

Like an unknown rock singer, he had shot straight into the charts. It brought home to him that modern art like rock'n'roll was essentially about attitudes. It didn't require manual skills developed over years of study and apprenticeship. The ingredient that enabled someone to do it successfully was to have the right approach. It was all about ideas and the ideas were judged in terms of their relevance.

The great advantage of this was that an individual artist could have quick and easy accessibility. He didn't have to be knocking on the door for years building up skills.

"Good rock music has nothing to do with manual ability: it is all to do with attitudes. All tunes are simply twelve bar blues organised in various ways. One is better than another because it has the right approach, what black musicians in America call soul.

"We hadn't needed any musical skills to start playing rock'n'roll. If you could get hold of a guitar and learn three chords you were off.

"I could see that it was going to be similar with modern art. The only rule was that you had to *know* what you were doing and you had to know where and what it related to. If you got your attitudes right you could make work that was kosher — even with the most limited skills.

"One great validating reason for modern art was the fact that anyone who had a commitment to art could immediately get involved. It afforded easy access to art."

His two small three-dimensional constructions had given him a foot in the door. But they were not what he wanted to continue doing. The experience with Farrell convinced him that his real affinity was with painting. What he lacked was a philosophy that would give him a rationale for doing it.

The pinball machine and the torso were in fact two-dimensional objects bent out into three-dimensional shapes. The logic in a painting would be to reverse the process. Which is what he did. He folded out and painted flat on canvas — like animal skins on a wall — a number of very recognisable three-dimensional consumer items: a box of matches, a HB ice cream carton, a Brillo box. They became visual puns emphasising Clement Greenberg's theory that a painting was simply a two-dimensional surface.

"Greenberg was preaching in New York about flatness and the integrity of the two-dimensional surface. All this filtered into ideas I'd absorbed from architecture about less being more and form following function. I felt it was an appropriate stepping-off point for me. But I doubt if anyone understood this at the time."

As a variation on the idea, he also painted a magnification of a razor blade — an object so flat that it had no depth.

Dublin in the 1960s had only two commercial galleries — the David (original Ritchie) Hendriks and the Dawson — both of which were fully committed to the more established names. But Brown Thomas department store now opened a small gallery adjoining its *haute couture* room. Ballagh was one of the newcomers invited to exhibit at the first show in February 1968. The others were Colin Harrison, Tim Booth, Brian Ferran, Shaun Davey, Frank Lee Cooper, Paul Mosse, Anthony O'Brien and Michael O'Sullivan, with whom he had sketched as a student.

The Brown Thomas Gallery under Amanda Douglas was to provide a venue for a burgeoning group of artists who had only been able to show annually at the Living Art. It was the beginning of an overdue opening-up of the market for art in Dublin.

A young artist had once called on Leo Smith at the Dawson and told him he'd be interested in showing at his gallery.

"*You* would be interested in showing in *my* gallery!" Smith exclaimed. "Maybe in two or three years I *may* consider looking at your work. *You* don't choose me. *I* choose you."

A pun on flatness. The controversial *Blade,* used as a backdrop for a Judy Geeson and Des Cave bed scene in Lee Dunne's banned movie *Paddy.* Acrylic on canvas, 72 x 36.

Ballagh's paintings in the Brown Thomas show — the blade, the matchbox and the ice-cream carton — were welcomed by Dorothy Walker as offering "a cool detached rendering of an article from everyday life, making the most of its aesthetic qualities and introducing the necessary cold-water shock to make us look at it by painting it very much larger than life-size and, in the case of the ice-cream pack and matchbox, by portraying them unfolded, flat upon the canvas."

The Arts Council provoked an uproar by paying £130 for the blade (later used as decor for a bed scene in Lee Dunne's banned movie *Paddy).*

"On what grounds?" demanded Quidnunc in the *Irish Times.* "I'm all with the Arts Council in the purchase of Michael O'Sullivan's *Triptych* but when I think of some of the fine Irish artists whose work was unsold at the last Hendriks group exhibition, I began to wonder if the tail is wagging the Arts Council dog."

Ballagh wasn't worried. He had sold his first painting.

"It's terribly important for artists to get an official clap on the back very early on even if it doesn't mean much financially. It builds up your confidence at a time when you are very vulnerable."

All his early paintings were exercises in problem solving: purely formal experiments in putting into practice tricks about masking tape and acrylic paint that he had learned from Farrell. He was discovering how to paint as he went along.

"I found the simplest things difficult. Like finding out how to put on a bit of masking tape and then stopping the paint seeping underneath. All sorts of elementary problems like that had to be solved."

Already he had caught the attention of an influential patron. Sir Basil Goulding, who opened the Brown Thomas show, shortly afterwards commissioned him to paint three large murals for the new Fitzwilton headquarters.

It was a chance to put into practice theories he'd developed as an architectural student about the function of art in relation to buildings. He was attracted by Fernand Leger's claim that art was for the people and that the only validity for abstract art was when it was used in an architectural context: the building and the people using the building gave the work a context. The only role the work had to perform was to provide light and colour.

But the murals turned out to be much more than a purely formal experiment along these lines. By basing them on shapes that seemed to be maps but in fact were purely abstract he was making a statement: the implication was that political boundaries were as arbitrary as the way an artist makes lines.

On a deeper level lay the pop concept of art being cool and detached and independent of the hand of the artist. All the shapes were arrived at in the manner of ink-blots. The choice of colour in each was decided by the throw of a dice. Almost every option was determined by the laws of chance.

Goulding was delighted with the effect even if he was unaware of the philosophy that had created it.

"You got the deep blue satisfyingly deep and right; and the weight of the grid-lines; and, with immense discrimination, the colour counterpoint of the land masses," he wrote in a letter of thanks.

"Altogether I find myself extremely complimented and very proud of my good judgement in feeling sure of your prowess . . . I shall be finding myself excuses to visit people working in the Ballagh area, and will probably be mooning about there of an evening after they have gone."

A smaller 4 foot by 4 foot treatment of the map series — the murals were 7 foot by 16 foot 4 inches — won an honourable mention in the under-25 section at the 1968 Living Art.

He had been working on a series of diamond-shaped canvasses using black outlines and masking techniques to create purely abstract patterns. One of these diamonds was also shown at the Living Art, another at the annual Belfast Open Show which ran from September 12 to October 19.

On October 5, 1968, about 2,000 supporters of the Civil Rights movement took part in a banned march through Derry in support of their demands for equal opportunities for Catholics and an end to sectarian discrimination against Catholics in housing, jobs and education.

On reaching Craigavon Bridge they were baton-charged by the Royal Ulster Constabulary. Republican Labour MP Gerry Fitt was among the 96 injured and taken to the nearby Altnagelvin Hospital.

As the marchers turned back in panic and tried to disperse down Duke Street they ran into another baton charge. That night barricades went up in the Catholic Bogside. The spiral of violence that led to the North's toubles had begun.

Ballagh watched it all on television. He saw the bloodied Gerry Fitt being led away. He saw women being beaten down by helmeted policemen. Yet while the North's minority took to the streets, he was exhibiting a diamond painting in Belfast.

He was never to paint another abstract.

4

He never fully went along with the Modernist cult of art for art's sake. The formalism of his early work was a stepping stone towards developing the skills and the language to make statements of his own through art. Now he felt driven to create a series of images that were to be a direct expression of his reaction to violence in a world turned into a global village by television.

"I was naive enough to think that I was somehow or other going to be the first artist to succeed in bringing art and politics together in a meaningful way."

He had been reading Marx and Marcuse and particularly Connolly — a socialist friend, Brian Trench, remembers that he took to wearing a Connolly badge at this time — and was convinced that workers in both North and South were about to make common cause in bringing about a 32-county socialist republic. His art was to be in the vanguard in changing society.

But he had no time for the archaic aesthetics of Sinn Fein activists whose idea of revolutionary art was little more than social realism *as Gaeilge.*

Through his reading of Che Guevara's essays *Man and Socialism in Cuba* and articles in magazines he received from Cuba, he was aware of attempts being made there to merge social realism with the brash techniques of American advertising layouts: political art made accessible to the masses through commercial art.

This was in tune with the pop vocabulary he had been building up. It provided a natural voice for his sense of outrage over the injustice in the North, the barbarism of Vietnam and the indignity of unemployment (which he had experienced firsthand in the dole queues in Gardiner Street).

Combining acrylic paint, on canvas and plywood, with a silk-screen treatment of photographs taken from newspapers and magazines, he devised multiple images of marchers, refugees, burning Vietnamese monks and South American firing squads: an iconography of the social consciousness of the 1960s.

The marrying of abstract hard-edge techniques to simple figurative ideas led him to a style of painting that was both an honest response to his own experience and something completely new in Irish art.

"For the first time I'd really painted something I thought of as my own. Not that I didn't think of my earlier paintings as my own. But I had been unable in them to get at things I wanted to say."

The works — twenty in all, including graphics, and entitled simply *Series 4* – formed his first one-man show, which was opened by Dr Conor Cruise O'Brien at the Brown Thomas Gallery on July 15 1969.

The North erupts. Catholics take to the streets in Derry's Bogside. The violence has been a recurring theme in his art.

This was before the lines had finally been drawn in the North. Civil Rights were the issue rather than the military ovethrow of British rule. Politics was still possible. The bullet and the bomb had not yet replaced the ballot as the weapon of change. The IRA were still waiting in the wings for an opportunity to exploit the situation — soon to be handed to them with internment. The split that led to the formation of the Provos had not even been mooted.

It was not unusual then to find Dr Cruise O'Brien associating himself with the radical left. He articulated the liberal concerns of the decade.

"Here are the symbolic disasters of our time," he said of Ballagh's *Series 4.* "Here too is that efficient impersonality of the modern media, which brings us visually so close to the terrible event, while at the same time insulating us from it in feeling.

"Robert Ballagh's burning Buddhist monk is seen for a moment on a television screen, yet the screen seems at the same time to be a magic lantern: the eye that has to see the monk had at the same time the integrity of a child's vision: the intensity of the image relives, actually increased by the reflected coolness of the interesting medium . . .

"The Artist's vision has in common with other human qualities —

Repetitive use of silkscreened photographs. *Series 4* paintings of marchers. 50 x 50.

with wit and humour for example — the fact that it represents a mysterious reserve of power, resembles I think, what Keats meant by negative capability.

"This has little to do with rationality — in the short-term sense for it can often seem highly irrational — but it is the quality in man which resists pinning down, which contains the capacity for a creative and surprising jump.

"Man in the past has mastered forces which on any obvious calculation ought to have mastered him. The forces which he now must master, if he is not to destroy himself, are in himself and in the society which he has made and is making.

"The struggle of self-adaptation for survival is not only reflected, but is actually going on in the world of art and here before our eyes, in the first exhibition of an exceptionally gifted, thoughtful young artist, Robert Ballagh."

Critical reaction concurred with O'Brien's judgement. "Quite the most striking and impressive first one-man show by an Irish painter for years," proclaimed Raymond Gallagher in the *Irish Press.* "He has robbed cinema of style and technique and moulded them to the static frame and silent wall," commented the *Evening Press.* "It is not too much to say that he has succeeded in making this transmutation with something not far short of genius."

Dorothy Walker marvelled that a young artist could be both so committed and yet able to exercise such impressive control of his medium. "He has taken the Pop technique of repetitive use of a silk-screened photograph, and developed the theme in an essentially original manner which I have not seen done anywhere before."

Bruce Arnold in the *Sunday Independent* regarded the majority of the paintings as already half-way to being universal statements of man's condition. But he thought their success might depend on the viewer's familiarity with the original material, something that might be lacking in a few of the images.

Brian Fallon in the *Irish Times* was a lone dissenter. He readily conceded that Ballagh was "inventive enough, at least technically, and daring enough in a conventional way. He is bright and breezy and knows the value of topicality and entertainment. His colour sense is keen, his taste sure."

But the hard-edge style with figurative connotations achieved "purely a surface resonance, and belongs as much to decorative and commercial art as to painting." The silkscreen process was "dangerously close to formula art". Fallon concluded with a pat generalisation that "most young artists today have any number of techniques at their fingertips, but are sometimes short on vision. With not a lot to say, they have a burning desire to say it, and a wide vocabulary for so doing."

Not for the last time Ballagh found the very effects he had sought to achieve — the surface resonance and the affinity to commercial art — being misunderstood and dismissed as shortcomings.

But public recognition reassured him. He was chosen to represent Ireland at the Paris Biennale with three paintings from the *Series 4.* He shared the Carroll's prize with Colin Harrison at the Irish Exhibition of Living Art in 1969.

The huge Stalinesque Museum of Modern Art on the Avenue Wilson, which housed the Paris Biennale, seemed remote from the nightmare that was engulfing the North. The only politics that mattered here was the politics of art.

"It was a real horse-trading affair. People kept robbing the best places to hang their work. Our commissaire general, the painter Cecil King, grabbed a good spot for me and made me stand there for hours while he collected my paintings and hung them. Then I had to stand there for hours more to make sure nobody whipped them down."

Brian King won the sculpture award for Ireland; Ballagh was edged out for the painting award by Juhani Linnovaara from Finland.

It was a salutary initiation to the wheeling dealing rites of international art.

"We'd been given strict instructions as to the maximum size of canvas, which I obeyed down to the last millimetre. My paintings were each 127 x 127 cms. Then John Walker arrived from England with an enormous canvas 266 x 670 cms. He simply ignored the rules and got away with it."

More than anything else the Biennale was a chance to make friendships. Ironically the most lasting of these was to be with a fellow Dubliner. Kieran Hickey had been chosen to represent Ireland in film with *Faithful Departed,* an elegiac evocation of James Joyce's Dublin created entirely from turn-of-the-century Robert French photographs which Hickey had discovered in the little-known Lawrence collection at the National Museum.

"We have movies in common," Hickey recalls. "Like me, the main source of his education had been the cinemas he attended rather than any schools. Too many people in Ireland would be ashamed to admit this. But he delighted in it.

"It was the first time I'd seen any of his paintings but I felt an immediate empathy with them. Here was someone working in a contemporary idiom which I could understand and using images of the world as I knew it.

"He was the most articulate artist I'd ever talked to — but without ever sounding as if he were explaining something he hadn't been able to put into his paintings."

The 1969 Irish Exhibition of Living Art was to open in Cork on August 21 — a gesture to draw attention to the lack of an adequate sized gallery in Dublin — and later move on to Belfast.

But the previous weekend CS gas was fired on Catholic youths who rioted in Derry following a provocative Apprentice Boys parade. Protestant mobs were allowed follow the police unhindered in the Catholic Bogside area, stoning houses. Defensive barricades were erected and the Republican Tricolour and the Socialist Starry Plough unfurled over "Free Derry".

Prime Minister Chichester-Clark called up 8,500 B-Specials — a Protestant reserve police force — for immediate duty. The Taoiseach Jack Lynch responded from Dublin by calling for the intervention of a UN peace force, claiming that the Stormont Government had lost all control. British Prime Minister James Callaghan then ordered in the Prince of Wales Own Regiment to take up security duty.

The Living Art could hardly remain unaffected by the enveloping sense of national emergency. Nor was it allowed to. Micheal Farrell announced that in protest he would not allow his work to be shown in Belfast. Ballagh was among a dozen fellow exhibitors to withdraw their work in support. As was Betty. Under her maiden name she had submitted a hard-edge abstract as part of a dare dreamed up by some of the artists' wives, notably Pat Farrell and Joan King. To all their surprise, it had been accepted.

Ballagh justified his withdrawal in an open letter to Norah McGuinness, president of the Living Art:

Dear Miss McGuinness,

I am writing to you to respectfully ask that my painting be withdrawn from the exhibition when it travels to Belfast. The reason for my delay in coming to this decision is that I wanted to avoid emotionalism especially of a kind tinged with Nationalism or religious fervour.

I would like this gesture to be accepted as a token of solidarity with the working-class people of the North in their recent struggle against fifty years of exploitive rule by the Unionist Government and their oppressive, often aggressive agents.

As an artist I feel naturally quite impotent in a situation such as the prevailing one. However, I recognise that just like any other worker the only weapon the artist can exercise for a cause he feels to be just is to withdraw his labour or in this case the product of his labour.

The argument has been raised that by this gesture the artist will deprive the very people he wishes to help of the opportunity of seeing something which is their right; nevertheless I feel that this is a negative appraisal of the situation. A more positive attitude is that he will deprive this much-tainted Stormont regime of a degree of credibility or cultural respectability; a regime which has consciously and consistently enlisted the basest of weapons, namely sectarianism, to maintain the status quo.

The easiest thing is to do nothing and so avoid making a decision, a decision to furnish a small but nonetheless valuable prop to Stormont.

All the withdrawn works were subsequently exhibited at a rival *Art and Conscience* show at 43 Kildare Street. The premises were readily made available by the newly-formed Citizens Committee, part of the nebulous operation that eventually led to the ousting from the Jack Lynch Government of Charles Haughey for alleged complicity in the import of arms for use by Catholics in Northern Ireland: he was subsequently cleared in the Arms Trial.

"Money was flooding indirectly through the Government into all sorts of organisations which had peripheral involvement with those who were later to form the Provos. I remember seeing radio equipment upstairs at No. 43 being prepared for despatch up North to become Radio Free Belfast."

Ballagh was spurred to join in the Living Art protest on account of Farrell's original gesture.

"But the more I thought it over in the following months the more I became convinced that an artist achieved nothing by withdrawing his art. It was a purely negative action. He ought instead to try to make a statement *with* his art."

Within months he was to get a chance to put this to the test.

1969 had been a remarkable year for him. He completed a major

commission, held his first one-man show, shared the Carroll's Prize
at the Living Art and represented his country abroad. All this within
two years of deciding to become a painter.

But there was little chance of him becoming over-confident.
He wasn't to sell another painting for over a year.

Going international. Betty and Robert with Joan King and
Brian King at the 1969 Paris Biennale, photographed on the
steps of the Museum of Modern Art, Avenue Wilson.

3

"Anyone who disowns any of their experience is foolish. Everything you do is of benefit to your development as a painter''

1

It's now over five months since he began the Downes portrait and he still hasn't painted any of the faces — the whole point of a conventional portrait.

"I'm nearly there," he assures me ruefully, "just a few shadows and all the surrounding areas will be complete."

But the shadows could take another three weeks. He will have to build them up with transparent glazes. And glazes take time to dry.

"A glaze is the most effective way of showing tones and shadows. You get an airiness and a lightness you wouldn't get by painting opaque colour wet onto wet. You can always see through a shadow. So it should not be a solid tone of pigment.

"I paint everything fairly flat at first and then introduce the glazes. That way when you glaze a shadow going from one place to another, it doesn't matter what intervenes along the way: it will still show through because the shadow is transparent."

The modern extension of the schoolhouse was originally on the same flat plane as the stonework. But by using this technique he has been able to make it seem to recede dramatically; the effect is three-dimensional.

"Of course basically it's no more honest than painting a shadow with solid opaque pigment. It's all an illusion. It *looks* more truthful rather than *is* more truthful."

It's not something he can rush. It has to be built up slowly. To get a dark tone might require laying down up to ten glazes. This would become too muddy and patchy if he tried to do it quickly all in one go.

The technique is not unlike the way a water-colourist would work,

Finding the right grouping. Contact prints of the Downes family provide a variety of compositional options for the portrait.

overlaying a wash of water-colour and building up wash upon wash to achieve a layered effect. But water-colour, being water-based, dries quickly. A glaze can't be touched for 18 hours after it has been laid on, even using a special resin to accelerate drying.

"It's time-consuming. If you've an area with twelve layers of glaze, you're talking of up to 20 days.

"But at least if you make a mistake, it's easy to change. If you put down a shadow glaze and it doesn't look right, you can simply wipe it off and start again."

Putting off doing the faces is not the gamble it seems. He has hundreds of photographs to work from. The likenesses have already been worked out in meticulously scaled drawings — the way an architect draws up plans for a building. Nothing in fact is left to chance in a Ballagh painting.

"I used a camera rather than make sketches because it has such a greedy eye. It picks up details you might not notice yourself. And it does away with the stiffness of people having to pose for you. I take so many shots they stop being aware of me.

"I like to have more information about a subject than I ever need. I can delete what I don't need afterwards. If you work from sketches, you tend to be selective before the painting even starts."

There's nothing arty about his camerawork for portraits. It's purely a means to an end.

"I'm not creating aesthetic images. I'm simply collecting data. So it's always in black-and-white. And I use a lot of flash. This flattens the image and gives much stronger shadows, which are more useful for turning into paint. If I was taking photographs to stand on their own merit I would always use natural light rather than a flash because you get a more natural picture that way."

A camera only shows the surface of reality. Which makes it a natural tool for a portrait. Because a portrait is about surface reality too.

"To a large extent that is all we can know about another person. I wouldn't presume to know a subject's deepest doubts and fears. All I have to go on is the external evidence.

"The world perceives us by what we've done and by what we've gathered around ourselves. The way we clothe ourselves in every sense of the word. This is the area I concentrate on in a portrait. As Ernst Thoms, an early twentieth century German realist painter said, we have painted inwards from the outside!

"I'm not the kind of painter who tries to capture the soul in the face. The whole picture will convey many different facets of the subject."

A Ballagh portrait becomes a visual inventory of a person's life. With Hugh Leonard, James Plunkett, Bernadette Greevy, Noel Browne or Charles Haughey, the approach works easily because they are well-known. The references can be readily recognised and understood. The challenge in the Downes portrait is to paint someone without a public image. It is the first time he has attempted to express something that is essentially private.

There couldn't be any short cuts this time. It wouldn't really have done to put a loaf of bread under Desmond's arm in reference to the family bakery business.

The association with Gainsborough's *Mr and Mrs Andrews* imbues the particular subject with a general significance. The portrait becomes a social statement. It's a device he has used before in many different variations: opening eyes to the present by referring to the past.

Pop art showed that an image could take on a new dimension by being lifted out of its familiar context. If this applied to a Coke bottle or a Campbell's soup can (to say nothing of a HB ice cream box or a Brillo carton) it ought to apply with equal force to a renowned art image.

But by its very nature it is an approach that makes considerable demands on his skill and discipline as a painter.

"It was alright in the early 1970s when my references were to a Lichtenstein or a Warhol. But now I'm working in the language used by Vermeer, Velazquez and Gainsborough. I have to try and match up their standards. It's not something you can dash off in a few days. You are inviting very demanding comparisons."

He finds he is taking longer and longer over each painting.

"I think what you put into a painting shows through. If you lavish it with care and attention, this will imbue it with some kind of aura that affects the observer, even though he mightn't know why."

Perhaps it's the Protestant work ethic: if something is worth doing, it is worth doing well.

"Nothing would frustrate me more in five years time than to see this portrait and spot a passage that I'd rushed off through impatience and to realise that if I'd spent another week on it it would have looked better."

That's always a daunting aspect of being a painter. A surgeon buries his mistakes. A painter's are hung on a wall and preserved in museums.

"I suppose I've changed as my work has changed. I wouldn't have had the patience to make pictures like this ten years ago. But I wouldn't have had the skills either. Then I couldn't wait to get each painting out of my system and to move on to the next.

"I think I'm painting now like I'd always have liked to paint if I'd been able. But that's not to say that I regard my early work as a courageous failure. I very consciously never tried to do something I couldn't achieve correctly within the limits of my ability at the time."

All his early paintings look crisp and clean. They didn't set huge problems to solve. But the few problems they set he was able to solve adequately so that the picture could stand in its own right as a finished object. He never tried to extend it beyond what he could do so that it looked messy or inadequate.

"Of course you must never get complacent and stay within the same tried technique. You've got to keep extending it gradually but always within the limits of your skills. That way you leave a body of works all of which have this finished look. When you look at them years later you don't feel embarrassed. They work within their own limits and intentions."

2

"We don't look at slides, Monsieur."

Nobody at the Basle Art Fair wanted to know him. It was really only a place for dealers and gallery owners to get together. Artists didn't belong. He had been there four days without making a single contact.

"It was like a cultural Spring Show. All the galleries had their stands. It was the whole commercial side of international art."

Cecil King had advised him to give it a try. His first show in New York had been called off at the last moment. It would be several months before his next show at the David Hendriks. He had to find somewhere quick to sell a few paintings and pay his bills. His last £100 had gone on an excursion return ticket.

He approached yet another stand. The Galerie des Quatres Mouvements in Paris.

"Would you like to see my slides?"

"Wait one moment."

He waited at the desk for twenty minutes while a leisurely discussion went on.

"I was perspiring and feeling wretched. Every moment I had to gulp down my impulse to tell them what to do with the gallery."

Eventually someone came over to him and shuffled quickly through the slides, putting a pile to one side.

"Are these for sale?"

"Yes"

"If we buy them, we'll expect fifty per cent reduction."

"What you do mean?"

"That's the standard arrangement. Our offer is two thousand, five hundred. You have until four o'clock to make up your mind."

He had nobody to turn to for advice. He went away to have a beer and a sausage. He waited until four and went back to the stand.

"It's a deal."

It was as if he had uttered a magic password. Doors suddenly began to open. He was introduced to Rudolf Jaggli and offered a show at the Aktionsgalerie in Bern. Nicholas Treadwell invited him to take part in a group show at his London Gallery. Within two years he had thirteen exhibitions throughout Europe.

He made this breakthrough into the international circuit with a series of paintings of people looking at paintings which he had started in 1972. They were a fundamental departure from the overtly political themes which dominated his first one-man show in 1969.

Then the issues in Ireland had seemed clear-cut. The Stormont Government and the B-Specials constituted a repressive regime. The Catholic minority in the North were being denied basic human rights. But the ideological rights and wrongs had become blurred by the resurgence of the outlawed Irish Republican Army, its morale boosted by a flow of funds and arms from American sympathisers.

IRA activists had participated in the early Civil Rights marches merely as stewards. But now, impatient with the tactic of civil disobedience and parliamentary pressure, the Northern command — to become known as the Provisionals — split with the more socialist elements in the movement — henceforth the Officials — and reverted to the traditional role of militant offensive against all aspects of the British presence in the North.

The Stormont Government retaliated by introducing internment without trial, which had the predictable effect of strengthening the Provos through further alienation of the Catholic community.

"There were no longer any obvious political options Robert felt he could identify with," remembers Brian Trench, a socialist journalist who has been one of his closest political friends since the mid-1960s. "His last overtly political work was a cover for *The Worker* in 1972. I think by then he had come to believe that an artist's political perspective was expressed more in terms of the way he worked than in direct identification with any view."

Withdrawing from the Living Art in Belfast in 1969 had set him thinking about the function of art and the relationship between the artist and society.

Even at the time he had doubted the effectiveness of the gesture. The essential power of art lay in the fact that it was a form of communication. Withdrawing it from an exhibition didn't make ideological sense. To be effective it had to be seen: it had to circulate as widely as possible.

He reversed his position at the first possible opportunity, accepting an Arts Council invitation to represent Ireland in the Celtic Triangle, a touring show of work by young artists from Scotland, Wales and Ireland that would be seen in Belfast and Derry as well as in centres in other countries.

He decided that the challenge would be to make paintings that would have some immediate relevance to the situation in the North. His research led him to Goya's *The Third of May*, Delacroix's *Liberty at the Barricades* and David's *The Rape of the Sabines.*

"The statement they were making about their time seemed exactly the kind of statement I wanted to make about my own."

He considered ways in which the images might be adapted. Picasso had already used *The Third of May* to make a comment on the Korean War. But this had involved altering the structure of Goya's painting. He decided to leave the structure the same but modernise the style. The message would take on a dramatic contemporary meaning by being expressed in a hard-edge black line Pop Art language.

David painted *The Rape of the Sabines* in the context of the internecine fighting after the French Revolution. The gesture of the women interposing themselves between the Romans and the Sabines was a plea for an end to sectarian strife that could readily be updated to apply to Protestants and Catholics in the North.

Goya's *Third of May*. A celebrated 19th-Century image of
repression provides the structure for a contemporary Pop Art
response to violence in Northern Ireland. The original for the
Ballagh version reproduced on page 36.

The more he pored over reproductions of these paintings the
more they seemed to merge with the images of violence in the North
he saw every evening on the television news.

Seamus Heaney made a similar connection in terms of poetry. In
August 1969 he saw the Goya painting *The Third of May* at the
Prado in Madrid. That night he turned on the TV in his hotel room
to see B-Specials rampaging up the Catholic Falls Road. For a
while he toyed with counterpointing the two images of violence in a
poem. Some months later he came across Ballagh's painting at the
Celtic Triangle show. He thought it intriguing that two Irish artists
in two different disciplines had thought of using the same Spanish
image of oppression in exactly the same association.

"Seamus understood very early on what my painting was about:
that it wasn't just a classical pastiche."

Critics were less perceptive. "Cartoonist send-up of famous paintings," complained the *Irish Times,* while *The Scotsman* observed that "Robert Ballagh, presumably in some kind of revolt, reduces masterpieces by Goya, Delacroix and Poussin (*sic*) to the basic terms found in comic-strip procedures."

He had expected a row in Belfast, particularly with *Liberty at the Barricades* — a large eight feet by six feet canvas showing Liberty waving a bright red flag — which was displayed in the window of the Arts Council Gallery immediately behind City Hall.

But in four weeks there was only one protest — from a woman outraged not at the political content but by the "indecency" of Liberty's bared breast.

The catalogue rather than the actual paintings provoked minor controversy in Dublin. He had written a note which stated: "These paintings are inspired by recent events in my country." But the words "recent" and "in my country" were omitted.

Before the opening at the Municipal Gallery he was asked not to distribute a pamphlet in which reproductions of his versions of The Third of May, Liberty at the Barricades and The Rape of the Sabines were printed beside photographs of bloody confrontations at Burntollet, Bogside and Derry in 1969. The accompanying text proclaimed: "These pictures are dedicated to those who struggle to create a 32-county Socialist republic in Ireland."

This experience taught him an important truth about politically motivated art: that because of the nature of the system by which art is put on show it is unlikely to change anything overnight.

"My paintings had been exposed to an elite art audience. They didn't get beyond that. Any political impact art has must inevitably be slow, like the erosion caused by water dripping on a stone."

In the years to follow they were to become among the most quoted images in Irish art. *The Third of May* is on the cover of the new history textbook for secondary schools. N. Glendenning reproduces it in his definitive study *Goya and His Critics* as drawing a striking parallel "between the presence of the French troops on Spanish soil in 1808 and English troops in Ireland in the 1970s."

3

Political art wasn't paying any bills. He had sold nothing since his *Series 4* success in 1969. He had a wife and two-year-old baby daughter to support. He went on the dole. Then took a job as a postman, for a while delivering letters on his own street. A commission to create screens for a cafeteria in the new University College Dublin complex at Belfield came as a lifeline.

The brief from architect Robin Walker, his one-time lecturer at Bolton Street, would have pleased Leger. Just bright colours and shapes. But the patterns would have to make sense no matter what way the screens were rearranged.

His job was to draw up working plans and supervise the actual painting, which would be done by professional decorators.

"We were using a beautiful clean Douglas fir plywood with attractive graining. It seemed a shame to paint it over. So I specified polyurethane stains which were just coming on the market. I wanted the wood to shine through the colour."

He was met by an elderly man in white overalls poring over his elaborate specifications for the masking-off of the shapes.

"This masking is a terrible nuisance. Are you sure you want me to use it?"

"Well, if you can manage as well without it . . . "

"No trouble."

The man dipped a brush into a can and with a quick whirl of his wrist painted a clean circle straight off without the suggestion of a dribble.

So began an invaluable apprenticeship. The man took a delight in demonstrating the tricks of his craft. Ballagh stood back enthralled. It was like being a child again watching the man painting the cinema signs.

"I picked up from him the kind of intuitive skills that you could never get in books. They have to be passed on. They're all in the shake of a wrist, the slant of a hand. You have to see it being done before you can do it yourself."

Like using a seagull's feather for marbling. The trick is to paint wet into wet. This produces a blotchy effect. The feather is then used to flick on a thin paint which simulates the white striation that distinguishes marble. The final touch, just when it is getting a little dry, is to dip a hand in turps and flick it over the paint.

Another trick, which in fact dates back to the Renaissance, enabled Ballagh to create the illusion of wood grain in *Homage to David*.

He mentioned that he was finding it tedious to hand-paint each

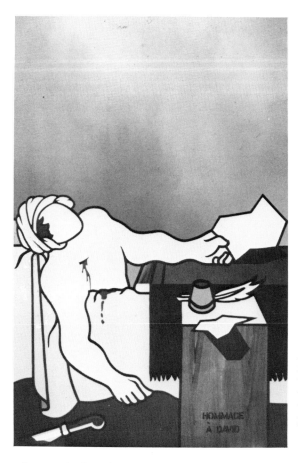

Neo-classical homage. Reworkings of *Turkish Bath* by Ingres, *Death of Marat* by David. Acrylic on canvas, 72 x 72, 60 x 48.

tiny grain in a large area of wood in the picture.

"Ah, now, shouldn't you be using the scumble for that?"

"Scumble?"

"We use it for the false grain on the doors of Corporation houses."

It's the opposite of a modern paint, which is manufactured to run together as it is applied with a brush: with scumble paint every hair line mark of the brush stays separate.

Experience gained from commissioned work throughout his career has fed back into his other work. This is one reason why he refuses to make any distinction between the two. They are simply different forms of problem-solving. He resents the conventional

prejudice that commissioned work is in some way "inferior" to an artist's "own" work.

"Anyone who disowns any of their experience is foolish. Everything you do is of benefit to your development as a painter."

While researching *The Rape of the Sabines* he had become intrigued by the career of David, discovering that he was a key figure in democratising the arts in the aftermath of the French Revolution. He became the equivalent to a Minister for Culture and was responsible for opening up the Louvre to the public for the first time.

"His painting of the assassination of his friend Marat in a bath ranks among the finest personal and political gestures in art. My stylised version was intended simply as a homage to him."

He felt drawn to the whole neo-classical tradition. There was a cleanness and purposefulness about it that attracted him. With growing confidence he took on the challenge of one of the *tour-de-force* works of the period, the huge circular Ingres *Turkish Bath* in which the 80-year-old painter remembered with sensual relish all the women in his life.

Tribute to Jacques Louis David, making its impact with the shocking red of the blood against the soft grey background, was shown at the 1970 Living Art, *Turkish Bath* at the Oireachtas, where it received a thumbs-down from the *Irish Times* for being "not far from the schematized drawing from a *Teach-Yourself-Art-Appreciation* handbook."

Ballagh remembers thinking it odd that an avowedly Pop painting should be criticised for the automatic look that is the very hallmark of Pop Art.

He might not have shocked Belfast with his politics, but it turned out that he had made a considerable impression there with his art. He was chosen as the first winner of the new Alice Berger Hammerschlag Award, established in the North to provide emerging young artists with, as chairman T.P. Flanagan put it, "anything that a creative talented artist might require to accomplish his work."

With Ballagh it provided the means to go to New York for the first time.

Almost the first gallery he went into on 52nd Avenue featured a large exhibition devoted entirely to different interpretations of the Ingres *Turkish Bath.* Variations on David's *Death of Marat* were on show at the Lerner Heller on Madison, where he was later offered an exhibition.

It was a timely reminder that in art nothing is ever new.

He spent much of his time at the Museum of Modern Art marvelling at the sheer scale and energy of Jackson Pollock and Frank Stella, whose paintings he had previously known only in reproduction.

He began to take stock of his own art: to work out where he was going.

If he had learned anything, it was that what matters in painting is not just the actual painting but the context in which it is perceived.

The fact that art was made for the elite audience inevitably conditioned what it could say. Art by its very nature was political quite apart from its content: at every stage it was a product of the interplay of social and economic as well as personal and individual forces.

He returned to Ireland determined to confront this truth: that way his painting might become like a Trojan Horse, challenging the suppositions of the gallery-dealer-critic system from within.

His first one-man show with David Hendriks in May 1971 systematically set out to introduce low art materials into a fine art setting. He used dyed nylon fur, phoney leopardskin and imitation wood panels as framings for magnified images of iced caramels, liquorice allsorts, gobstoppers, dolly mixtures, chocolate beans and cakes: visual puns on popular taste. Send-ups of conventional "art" pictures of stags and ducks, which people are apt to hang in their drawing rooms, completed the effect.

The catalogue carried what amount to a manifesto:

"I am convinced that when future archaeologists browse over the bones of our epoch, they will unquestioningly accept the artefacts, which presently make up the sub-culture of the masses, to be truly representative of our culture; this in spite of the present elevation and perpetuation of an 'accepted' culture and the consequent low status of the mass art type.

"For the first time in history technology has made cheap mass production of artefacts for general dissemination possible. However, this technological advance, coupled with a retrograde social system, which reduces all things to a commodity level, has led to the production of a culture type, which arouses the basest aesthetic reasoning in people and stimulates this for profit. Unscrupulous producers dupe the naive into purchasing an ersatz luxury where nothing is as it seems: wood is plastic, fur is nylon and marble, printed paper.

"In these pictures, however, there is no attempt to create a kitsch art form which at best is intellectual slumming, rather I wish to present, without comment, the cultural reality of most people's lives."

He issued a press statement to hammer home the point:

"The pop artists claimed that they represented urban reality. In fact they created a capitalist realism in which they celebrated the advertising dream world displayed on the posters, hoardings and on the mass media.

"This creation of the ad-man has little to do with reality. Few people enjoy the Martini world of the TV commercial. The reality of most people's lives is in fact a domestic environment which is both crass and claustrophobic."

Both these statements serve more as an insight into the thinking that inspired his paintings than as an accurate description of what they were. Liquorice allsorts were hardly a symbol of the "crass and claustrophobic" reality of most people's lives nor were they an obvious example of "unscrupulous producers" duping the naive. Neither in this nor in any other show has his art ever been merely an illustration to an argument. The argument provides the stimulus to make a painting which then takes on a life of its own.

To coincide with the opening of the Hendriks show he contributed an article to *Hibernia* entitled *Socialism and the Artist* in which he reasoned that rather than propagate the socialist message in his work "the artist can play a more immediately useful and far less fallible role in the path to socialism by attacking the economic base within which he is forced to work. This base, namely the private gallery system, is not only exploitive of the artist, but also has tremendously damaging effects on art itself." Quite apart from putting the artist in a position of economic dependence, it binds him "to an elite and thus in consequence must effect the very content of his art... The artist to survive economically must consciously or unconsciously produce art which will appeal to the public provided to him by the dealer.

"This must be seen as a very vicious circle indeed, as far removed from the working class as can be . . . as it tends to push art into a peripheral position."

Before the article appeared and the night before the exhibition opened, he dropped a letter through Hendrik's letter-box which Hendriks kept until his death in 1983 but never discussed with him.

Dear David,

You will probably read with horror an essay of mine to be published, I believe, in the next issue of *Hibernia.* I would like to say, right now, that in this essay no personal invective is directed against you or any other individuals directly involved in art in Ireland.

When I was approached to submit my opinions for publication I baulked at the proposition as I felt that many people, whom I indeed respect, might be offended. Nevertheless I felt that to withhold my deeply committed beliefs would be terribly dishonest. As a socialist I believe that under capitalism everything is deformed; this is true in art as in economics. Capitalism is a tragically corrupt system that forces even honest and genuine individuals to capitulate to its cruel economic principles. The point I want to make is that it is the system that is corrupt not necessarily the people who administer it. I make no apologies for my beliefs, but as I direct no personal abuse against individuals, I hope that as an individual myself I might receive a similar treatment."

Immediately after the article appeared, *Hibernia's* editor John Mulcahy called at the gallery overlooking St Stephen's Green.

"Did you read it?" he asked Hendriks.

"Yes."

"What are you going to do about it?"

"Nothing."

Mulcahy seemed disappointed. "He obviously expected me to be furious and perhaps cancel the exhibition," Hendriks recalled. "That would have given him another juicy story."

Few, apart from Hendriks himself and Basil Goulding, who welcomed the show as "a cold nose up the arse", were prepared to make this distinction. The issue became confused in a row over personalities.

Bruce Arnold wondered facetiously how Ballagh could bring himself to exhibit in private galleries if he regarded the system as a "cock-eyed set-up".

Even critics who praised the paintings confessed to disliking them. Dorothy Walker thought that they pointed the finger so unerringly at the absurd horrors of our technical expertise "that I cannot imagine anyone wanting to buy them."

The *Glasgow Herald,* when they were shown with works by Cecil King and Patrick Collins at the Compass Gallery, expressed bafflement as to how "these presumably deliberately unpleasing paintings" pursued his stated argument.

The show had been anything but a financial success: which in a sense proved his case. But David Hendriks stood by him.

They had been introduced two years before by Robin Costello, who exhibited with Hendriks and had known Ballagh at Blackrock.

"David said nice things then but made no offers. It was almost as if you had to do your apprenticeship. You had to be in the Living Art and win a prize or two and only then might a gallery consider you. David started me off first in his Christmas group show in 1970 and only a year later did I qualify for a one-man show. Nowadays there are so many galleries, young artists get snapped up. But it was different then."

The Hendriks Gallery, as it was renamed after his death in 1983, is one of Dublin's oldest: the fact that it only opened its doors in 1956, soon after Hendriks moved there from Jamaica (one of his contemporaries at school had been the future Socialist Prime Minister Michael Manley), indicates how recent and how rapid has been the development of an art market in Ireland.

Through Hendriks' initiative in the 1960s, international art made its first real impact in Dublin, particularly with the pioneering Kinetic show in 1966. Even before the first Rosc in 1967 he had introduced work by Vasarely, Morellet, Albers, Calder, Soto, Le Parc, Arp, Cruz-Diez and Adami.

But even with his open approach he found Ballagh difficult to appreciate at first glance. "I'd seen his *Razor Blade* and couldn't understand how it was art. It was so flat and featureless. It was only later that I understood what he was getting at."

Yet clearly, at only 28, Ballagh already had the makings of a significant painter. The selection of five of his paintings for Rosc 71 confirmed this status. The razor blade, a map, The Third of May, the burning monk and liquorice allsorts in effect formed a mini-retrospective within the main exhibition.

5

These were heady days of political activism. He cooperated with painter John Vallely and the People's Democracy, the socialist movement founded in Queens University in 1968, in organising people's festivals — an attempt to generate cultural involvement in the political context of the North's troubles. There were exhibitions and stormy meetings with speakers like Bernadette Devlin at the Project Arts Centre in Abbey Street, then a focal point for committed art.

"You were convinced that the status quo couldn't survive. That in a year or two Ireland was going to be changed utterly. You felt you had to be everywhere at once. If I heard of an eviction or a protest

International Socialism 51

Ireland

Stylised portrait of the executed Socialist leader James Connolly, a cover design for *International Socialism.*

march I didn't know about, I'd be furious that I'd missed it."

Brian Trench asked him to design a cover for *International Socialism* in homage to James Connolly, the protégé of Engels who was executed after the suppression of the 1916 Rising in Dublin. He had previously painted the theme in the form of a pop ikon with four panels showing a silhouette of Connolly, a shattered pane of glass symbolising violent death, the Plough from the *Plough and the Stars* flag, and a silhouette of the workers riots in Dublin in 1913.

The Labour Party held it on approval for six months, unable to make up its mind about buying it. It now belongs to Sam Stephenson, a prominent Fianna Fail supporter and the architect responsible for some of Dublin's more controversial office blocks.

It was his last work using black outlines and a predominantly pop vocabulary, apart from a commission to celebrate the achievements of Dr. T.A. McLaughlin, one of the founders of the Electricity Supply Board, and a series of five writers' heads — Joyce, Shaw, Wilde, O'Casey and Behan — painted in circular frames and completed two years later for the new Tara hotel in London.

The black outline had threatened to become a style: and it was too closely associated with the English painter Patrick Caulfield. He didn't want to be typecast or bracketed with anyone else.

Gordon Lambert was on the advisory committee that recommended him for the ESB commission. "Let's try something imaginative instead of yet another representational bust," he urged his colleagues. "Let's give Robert Ballagh a free hand."

The content virtually dictated the form of the 17 foot by 7 foot mural: a dam, a power station, pylons and workers all had to be included. But he enjoyed the challenge of making a striking image from so tight a brief. The result is a blend of social realism and modern American graphics: the influence of his Cuban awareness is evident. "I don't think it was all that popular with the staff," says Lambert, "but it works very well in the foyer. It gives the public something to look at."

With the heads for the Tara hotel, the problem was the reverse: the specification was for as little detail as possible. He had to capture a likeness with minimal technique. The stylised approach was similar to that which he had used for the Connolly portrait, which had won the Arts Council's Douglas Hyde gold medal.

Dissent had been stirring within the Living Art. Young artists felt that it was not sufficiently responsive to change. Brian King was brought on to the committee to provide a measure of reform in 1971 but eventually the entire committee, led by Norah McGuinness, resigned and handed over the presidency to Brian King. She readily conceded that they had become too old and too much like an establishment. The Living Art, she announced, would be a contradiction in terms if it came to be regarded as representing the status quo. It ought constantly to renew itself.

True to the authoritarian nature of all revolutionary change, King promptly formed a new committee from his own group of friends, most of whom drank at Toners: Ballagh, Michael O'Sullivan, Charlie Harper, Erik van der Grijn and, representing Northern Ireland, Brian Ferran.

The first exhibition under the new regime proved to be a watershed. With performance art, sound art, installations, photo as art, video work and language art it anticipated the whole gamut of what was to become the art of the 1970s.

"We were all in our twenties. No holds were barred. No matter what anyone wanted to do, the more outrageous it was the better. We were trying to force a change which in fact was to take several years to percolate through."

Politicial ikon. Visual references to the 1913 lockout, the Starry Plough and shattered glass (a frequent Ballagh symbol for violent death) form a portrait of James Connolly. Acrylic on canvas, 60 x 40.

Irish artists living abroad were invited to contribute special works — Noel Sheridan in Australia, James Coleman in Milan, Les Levine and Brian O'Doherty in New York, and Sean O'Flynn in Paris.

Each member of the committee also undertook to attempt something totally different from their normal work.

Bloody Sunday haunted Ballagh's memory. On January 31, 1972, British troops had opened fire indiscriminately on Catholic marchers in Derry, killing thirteen. Mobs burned down the British embassy in Dublin in retaliation. But reaction since had been strangely muted.

"People seemed to have washed their hands of responsibility for doing anything. They had become apathetic to what was happening in the North.

"I felt that a gesture was needed to bring home to them what death in the streets really meant."

He chalked out on the concrete floor of Project the crude outline of thirteen bodies — the way police do after a murder. He then stained the floor boards with real blood supplied to him by a friend from Toners who worked in the city abattoir.

Guests at the opening of the Living Art at first walked gingerly around the outlines. But as the drink flowed, they forgot they were there. By the end of the evening all trace of the chalk marks had been trampled over: just as the memory of Bloody Sunday had been erased from the public consciousness.

It was a completely ephemeral art gesture. The only way it could be preserved was through photographs. It could not be diminished by becoming a commercial art object: no profit could be made from it.

"I think of all the political images I've made, it was the most effective."

The 1972 Living Art was a coming-of-age. It confirmed the emergence of a new generation of artists eager to embrace contemporary styles rather than meekly perpetuate the Connemara landscapes and rural themes that had come to typify Irish art. Their images were a response to a different reality — the reality of an outward-looking urban society. But it also confirmed the existence of an affluent new local market for art generated by the industrial transformation of the 1960s.

Basil Goulding and Gordon Lambert used the Contemporary Irish Art Society to mobilise this new wealth to acquire works by

One of thirteen figures outlined in chalk on the floor of Project to symbolise the victims of the Bloody Sunday atrocities. Living Art Exhibition, 1972.

Pouring animal blood on the floor of Project. A political art gesture that survived only in the form of photographic evidence.

living Irish artists for the Dublin Municipal Gallery which had no purchasing funds of its own. Eventually Goulding lost patience with the apathy of Dublin Corporation, which had legal responsibility for the gallery. He offered, through the Society, to acquire Ballagh's *Iced Caramels* for the Gallery — but only if the Corporation came up with half the price. A vote approving the necessary £150 was hurried through.

Once the precedent had been established, the Corporation in subsequent years approved ever-increasing sums for the Gallery, going up from £2,500 in 1972 to the present £30,000. Regrettably the Gallery has been less than enterprising in its use of the funds, in some years not even using up its full allotment.

As chief of the huge biscuit empire that included both Jacob's and Boland's, Lambert occupied a key position in Irish industry, a position emphasised by his directorships of various other companies, his role in the "Buy Irish" campaign in the 1960s and his continuing involvement as a council member both of the Irish Management Institute and the Confederation of Irish Industry.

But his commercial career, like Sir Basil's Goulding's, had been paralleled by an ever-increasing involvement in the arts. He was a board member of the Arts Council of Northern Ireland, a member of the international committee of the Museum of Modern Art in New York, a founder member of the Society of Designers in Ireland and a member of Project, Dublin Theatre Festival, Wexford Arts Centre Council, the Hugh Lane Municipal Gallery Advisory Committee, the Friends of the National Collection, the Fine Arts Advisory Board of the National College of Art and the Friends of the Wexford Opera Festival.

With his private collection of nearly two hundred paintings, sculptures, etchings, prints, drawings, gouaches and watercolours — which he began on his income as an accountant in the 1950s — he gave the lead to a whole new breed of art patrons who for the first time have made it possible for artists to live and sell in Ireland.

He had bought *Homage to David* in 1970 and had been involved in the *Iced Caramels* manoeuvre. He now approached Ballagh to paint his portrait. "I remembered his parents from our tennis club days," says Lambert, "but I'd never met Robert. I tended to veer away from his early work, particularly the packaging. I was so involved in marketing for Jacobs, I couldn't see what he was getting at. But I was soon won over by the whole speed and inventiveness of his

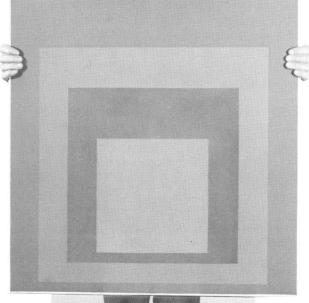
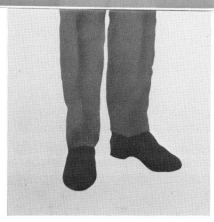

Portrait of Gordon Lambert. The idea of showing the subject holding an Albers led to a series of pictures of people looking at paintings. Acrylic and Silkscreen on canvas, 72 x 36.

development."

Ballagh decided to depict him in a pin-stripe businessman's suit but holding a large Albers abstract (which he copied from one in the Municipal Gallery). The figure was cut out rather than framed and the hands gripping the edge of the canvas were modelled in three-dimensional form. They were cast from Ballagh's own hands by Brian King, who was then using Micheal Farrell's studio in Sandycove — which made it a unique collaboration by three of Ireland's leading young artists.

The face caused problems. He hadn't yet developed the necessary figurative skills to capture a satisfactory likeness. After several attempts, he decided to silkscreen a photograph instead, a pop device which in fact enhanced the image.

He had stopped using black outlines but still followed the technique of masking off spaces before filling in the colours. Instead of flat colours he now used modulated tones to simulate the material of the clothes.

The concept of this portrait led logically to a series of pictures of people looking at paintings which became his next one-man show with David Hendriks.

He tried out the idea first with a back view of three people in a gallery studying one of his own paintings of marchers. He then felt emboldened to attempt the same approach with a Jackson Pollock.

Pastiche had always fascinated him. He impressed his mother by tossing off le Brocquys as a schoolboy. With the Chessmen he played rock variations on classical tunes. It was as if by osmosis he could become part of what he admired.

He didn't copy Jackson Pollock. He created an entirely new Pollock of his own. It was more difficult than anything he had attempted before. Pollock worked with oils, which are slow to dry, whereas he was using quick drying acrylics: this made it difficult to get the distinctive splash effect. But the result greatly impressed the American painter's biographer Francis O'Connor, who ranked it as the best of the many forgeries of Pollock he had examined — quite apart from being a striking work in its own right.

After Pollock no Modernist painter was safe from his tongue-in-cheek scrutiny. Using the panel format, originally developed purely as a means of making large paintings in the small room in Broadstone which he used as a studio up to 1970, he built up a virtual gallery of his own versions of Barnett Newman, Capogrossi,

Soulages, Gottleib, Stella, Lucio Fontana, Jasper Johns, Morris Louis, Franz Kline, Clyfford Still, Robert Motherwell, Bradley W. Tomlin and Ellsworth Kelly. He even ventured a few homages to Irish contemporaries — a Cecil King, a Micheal Farrell and a Patrick Scott.

The figures in each case were derived from photographs which he collected from newspapers and magazines. But he might take weeks before he found a figure standing in the right way. So he began taking his own photos with a second-hand Rolleicord. The need to solve a pressing problem yet again opened a door that was later to add a totally new dimension to his art.

The Hendriks show was a complete sell-out.The Arts Council gave a lead by paying £600 for the Jackson Pollock. Gordon Lambert bought the Fontana. Ronnie Tallon, the architect, purchased the Newman, King, Capogrossi, Soulages, Gotleib, Stella and Ballagh's own marchers on behalf of the Bank of Ireland collection.

Brue Arnold in the *Irish Independent* predicted that the Arts Council would "in five years or so, feel a certain prickle of embarrassment that they had been so rash." Brian Fallon in the *Irish Times* wouldn't "take bets on all this in ten years time, let alone fifty. Ballagh is almost too much a child of his time." But Blaithín Ó Ciobháin in the *Irish Press* proved a better prophet: "It is a great advance on last year's show and if he continues progressing at the rate of the past few years, he will be a formidable figure in the art world in the mid-1970s."

As a thank-you to Hendriks for his unwavering support Ballagh, with the connivance of Lambert, painted a surprise portrait of the dealer sitting with a painting in much the same style as Lambert's own portrait.

"The first I knew about it was when I came in and found it hanging over the mantelpiece," Hendriks recalled.

By responding to his own experience Ballagh had arrived at a style strikingly in tune with the New Realism vogue then dominant in international art. The Lerner Heller Gallery, with which he had established contact on his first visit to New York, now hastened to offer him a show, Heller himself flying to Dublin to see work in progress in his studio. But the show fell through. He was left with a pile of paintings and nowhere to show them.

Cecil King and Oliver Dowling, who was then exhibitions officer in the Arts Council, had suggested the trip to the Basle Art Fair.

He initially received so many rebuffs at Basle that he'd have come home if the excursion ticket hadn't obliged him to stay at least a week.

"I shudder to think what might have happened if I hadn't finally made contact with the Galerie des Quatre Mouvements."

The immediate consequence — apart from the welcome arrival of a banker's draft for £2,500 from Paris a week after his return — was participation in a group show on the theme "Portrayal of Betrayal" at the Nicholas Treadwell Gallery in London. All the artists taking part were invited to portray Treadwell, an ebullient extrovert who defied the conventional stereotype of a Bond Street dealer.

"The aim was to encourage a revival of portrait commissions," said Treadwell. "The result was an interesting comparison of styles of portrayal in the spirit of the 1970s."

Ballagh pictured him from the rear looking at a Magritte room — but in a way that he seemed to be actually inside the room itself.

Robert and Betty took in the London opening on their way overland to Bern for the one-man show at the Aktionsgalerie.

"We had all the paintings for the show tied up in bundles which had to go in the guard's van on the train. As we pulled out of a station on the French border I looked out the window and saw them all being left behind on the platform.

"When we arrived in Bern nobody could find out anything about them. They didn't turn up until a few hours before the opening. It was a panic experience trying to join all the panels together in time.

"The anti-climax was that a total of only *three* people then turned up. The opening coincided with the annual United Nations celebrity concert. We left for home the next morning convinced that it was my first and last European show."

But a cable from gallery owner Rudolf Jaggli awaited them in Dublin: there had been a virtual sell-out the following night. Not only that, but Isy Brachot, one of the biggest dealers in Belgium, had dropped in between trains and bought six paintings.

Within days Brachot himself wrote offering a show in Brussels.

It was only when Ballagh arrived over to hang the show that he realised what a breakthrough he had achieved.

The Brachot gallery occupied an entire building on the fashionable Avenue Louise. Each floor contained a separate gallery. There was even a special photographic department to record every painting going on exhibition and provide prints to magazines and newspapers.

"I realised I'd made the first division. They wouldn't even allow me to hang the paintings. A man called Maurice in a beautiful white uniform with Isy Brachot embroidered in gold took charge of all that.

"At the opening girls walked around with clipboards containing a complete dossier of my work.

"Maurice was at the door to greet me with the news that I'd alrady sold thirteen paintings. But I couldn't see any red spots when I went in. Then I noticed tiny plaques with the word "Vendu" hanging under the paintings.

"I invited all the Irish EEC crowd. But it was the Belgians who bought. The Irish, with the exception of one friend, didn't buy a drawing between them.

"My dearest painting fetched £700. But there was a show of work by Magritte, Delvaux and Gnoli in the ground floor gallery at which a small Magritte went for £70,000. I was within zeros of Magritte!"

They were the only Magrittes he saw in Brussels. The city had no proper Museum of Modern Art. The Palais des Beaux Arts was exclusively a showplace for the great masterpieces of Flemish art. It seemed extraordinary that Magritte should be so little represented in what had been his home city. He was to discover why when he returned for a second show two years later.

A young man who gave Betty and himself a lift back to their hotel after the opening of the second show invited them to lunch the next day. The address turned out to be a beautiful family residence in the district of Uccle. They were ushered into the living room. There was a Chagall over the fireplace, a Matisse beside the door and in a special alcove, five small Magrittes he had never seen reproduced anywhere.

"Ah, but he did them specially for us," Madam Oshinsky explained.

Magritte had been a regular at her Saturday night *soirées*. His friend Louis Scutinaire, who organised the Magritte retrospective at the Pompidou Centre in Paris, still came.

"We're meeting this Saturday. You must join us."

They established an immediate rapport with Scutinaire, who had a passion for the gothic novel.

"You must visit my home," said Scutinaire. "I want to hear all about Joseph Sheridan Le Fanu and Chapelizod."

Scutinaire's home was crammed with 60 or 70 Magrittes, including most of the works from the so-called *vache* (cow) period. These had been painted by Magritte in a pique. Paris regarded anyone from Brussels as a country cousin. He decided to live up to the title. He literally squeezed paint straight out of the tube onto the canvas, creating a series of works that were the antithesis of his normally meticulous technique: brash, vulgar images that bombed with the Paris critics, who pleaded plaintively for a return of "the Magritte of yore". Scutinaire then helped Magritte write a spoof biography entitled *Magritte of Yore.*

There was also work from Magritte's little-known Renoiresque period, painted in a beautiful sunny way as a counterbalance to the terror of the Second World War.

"Scutinaire even showed us the so-called pornographic drawings, which Magritte's widow had suppressed. They were more rude than porno. Magritte was very bourgeois. He went about in a bowler hat. The drawings have to be seen in that light."

Scutinaire was a somewhat eccentric host. No two guests were allowed try the same brand of beer — he was proud of the large variety of beers available in Belgium — and he himself always drank from the neck of the bottle like a peasant.

He noticed Betty rolling her own cigarettes.

"Would you roll one for me?"

She did.

He sniffed it expertly.

"Do you want a light?"

"No, no" he replied.

And he slowly ate the cigarette.

He was like a Magritte painting coming to life.

There is an obvious affinity between Ballagh and Magritte. Both share the same precise vision and both put a strong emphasis on content.

On being criticised once for not finishing out a painting, Magritte replied: "A painting needs to be only as good as is necessary to convey the idea. Any other effort spent on it is a waste of time."

Although Magritte's reputation has ebbed and flowed with changing taste, his influence is enduring. With Dali, he is one of the few artists to have influenced the way twentieth-century man sees the world. Movies and advertising are rich in images directly derived from his paintings.

But the visual puns and literary allusions in which Magritte delighted and to which Ballagh found himself increasingly drawn were taboo to Modernist art.

Ballagh had embarked initially on his series of people looking at paintings as an ironic comment on the affection of regarding art in terms of labels.

"People spoke of *a* Pollock or *a* Lichtenstein as if the names were some sort of house-style or brand label. They didn't really consider the actual works themselves. It was as if Modernism had become a new form of academicism."

But the series gradually developed into his own personal examination of Modernism.

"By the time I'd finished I'd more or less lost faith in a lot of the rules."

This growing sense of disillusionment is evident in subtle shifts in the presentation of the figures.

They turned into cut-outs in his 1975 Hendriks show, inspired by the cardboard Kodak lady he remembered seeing outside the chemist's shop in Ballsbridge when he was growing up. Then, by turning the figures around, he found he could comment on how a work by Leger, for instance, who saw himself as a people's painter, could finish up as the incongruous plaything of the idle rich. By 1975, in a work bought by the Ulster Museum, he was using flourescent tubes in a pastiche of the style of the American artist Dan Flavin.

"It had got to the audacious stage where friends would bet that I couldn't do so-and-so and I'd take them on. I'd have a crack at Picasso or Matisse or whoever."

Eventually he wrapped up the series by painting himself bending down to sign *The Third of May.*

He wasn't just signing off from the series.

He was signing off from Modernism.

4

"I've always had this hatred of style. Other painters deliberately cultivate brush strokes to give character to their painting. I feel compelled to remove them."

1

He has glazed in the final shadows of the Downes portrait. The canvas is almost dry.

"Handing over a picture is always a difficult moment for me. The subject has no idea what to expect. Whatever they may eventually come to think about it, their first glimpse is bound to be something of a shock."

Everyone has their own idea of how they look. They have their own way of seeing themselves and of wanting to be seen. This is why even a photograph can fail to catch a likeness to their satisfaction. They reject it subconsciously not because it isn't accurate but because it doesn't conform to their own image of themselves.

"I always insist on being free to paint a portrait in my own way. If people want a traditional academic likeness they're not going to come to me in the first place. They choose me because they're familiar with my work. They must accept the consequences.

"Of course I'll listen to their ideas and their preferences. If they want Aunt Mary's cat in the background I'll try to oblige. But I can't tolerate any interference.

"That's one of the reasons I refuse to let the subject see a portrait until it's finished. It's terribly dangerous to show anything half-way through. Because it's only human nature for people to feel obliged to make some comment. Even if it's only a throwaway remark. Like such and such doesn't look right. And you might spend a week trying to correct something that wasn't wrong in the first place."

A painted likeness is one person's impression of another rather than an automatic copy from life. If it showed exactly what was there

Getting a likeness. Scaled outline drawing of the Downes family. Already the automatic photographic copy from life is giving way to the artist's own abstracted version of the subject.

— like a photograph — it would in fact look untrue.

"If you're painting from a photograph you have to leave out many details. Because a painting places too much emphasis on everything. If you left in all the wrinkles that are actually there, the person would look like a prune. All painting is a form of abstraction."

Detail that the eye passes over in real life stands out in a painting. The eye normally focusses on a small area of its field of vision but a portrait is seen in total focus.

This can create a problem with hands as much as with faces. They tend to stand out in a painting. Yet most hands lack the beauty to survive close scrutiny. The fingers tend to be short rather than long and graceful. Advertising agencies get around the problem by hiring models with attractive hands. The artist has to make the best of what's there.

"I tend to paint them accurately at first and to work from that to make them presentable. With a single subject you can usually get rid of one hand altogether by putting it in a pocket or behind a book. But that's not possible in a group. It would look odd if all the hands were hidden away."

The challenge has been to contrive a way of arranging them so that they don't become too much of a distraction.

"I don't want them to upset the overall balance of the composition."

Every painting invariably reduces down to a series of decisions like this: an exercise in problem-solving not just in approach and composition but at every level down to the actual mixing of the paints.

By now he has developed the habit of opening a file as soon as he contemplates a painting. Each choice made in its preparation is noted down for further use.

He points to the canvas chair on which Margaret Downes is sitting.

"If I ever want to repeat that particular green I'll be able to look it up and recall exactly the formula of its composition."

Keeping records makes it easier afterwards to touch up paintings that become damaged or need to be restored, particularly now that he works in oils which, unlike acrylics, do not alter radically in the process of drying. The same mix will always produce more or less the same tone when applied to the canvas. With acrylics, which are water-based and dry rapidly, the colour might go through a whole tone change while drying.

"It never matches with what's there when you put it on first. You can't tell whether you've got it right until it dries."

He seldom uses acrylics now. He has gradually abandoned the medium in which he first made his name. The changeover to oils dates from his series of people looking at paintings. Any detail he employed before then had been fairly bland. He was using big areas of flat colour, which suited acrylics. They dried in a few minutes. They could be worked quickly. But this became a liability once he started turning around the figures in the series. Painting wet into wet to get the tones of the clothing was a hit or miss process. He couldn't paint faces that way. So he began introducing oil for areas that needed a little longer working time.

"I soon found that I had a much greater empathy for oils. I began phasing out acrylics from my repertoire. Acrylic paint is not really suited to figurative work. It becomes very dry looking when you do a lot of overlaying. By its very nature it's a flat, brash medium. It only came into its own with hard-edge abstraction in the 1960s."

But a fundamental contradiction in the Downes portrait — and in all his recent work — is that although painted entirely in oils, it has the same bland look of an acrylic painting. There is no trace of any brush strokes.

"People think I use a spray gun. But everything you see has been applied conventionally with a brush or a sponge or a roller. Not that I'm adverse to using a spray gun. I didn't use one at the start simply because I had no electricity and I then developed a way of painting which I grew to prefer to sprayed work.

"Spray paint looks all right on flat hardboard or plywood. But not on the pitted surface of canvas. When you blow paint onto canvas it only hits the tops of the hills. The hollows don't take it. Even though you spray over and over again, you still get a dusty look to it."

His early paintings in oils were essentially experiments in eliminating the tell-tale brush strokes.

"Gestural brush strokes give style to a painting. They are like handwriting. I equate style with fashion as being ephemeral and egotistical.

"If there is a constant in my work it is a desire for a clean look.

"To be meticulous and precise. To eliminate any physical mark of the artist's hand. When I began to paint figuratively, I very consciously sought to retain this characteristic."

He set aside half of each day for a series of figurative images of famous abstract painters as a means of getting to grips with the technical difficulties of working in oils. They were essentially practice works which he subsequently destroyed, apart from a study in green of Hans Hoffman and a silver portrait of Andy Warhol: both of these were exhibited in 1975, together with a blue Mona Lisa.

Out of this period of trial and error came one of his strangest and most potent — but also least known — images: a large 5 foot by 4 foot portrait of his six-year-old daughter Rachel pretending to be Marilyn Monroe. The juxtaposing of roles somehow captures the whole aura of vulnerability that surrounds the Monroe legend, the sense of sexiness set against innocence.

"My idea was to take someone who wouldn't understand any of the sexual connotations of the thing but would enjoy the theatricality of dressing up with wigs, false eye-lashes and make-up."

There is a romantic softness about the image not found in any of his other work, an effect heightened by the cinematic close-up format, which suggests a pin-up photo. But although he received offers of commissions to do repeats, it has remained a one-off idea.

"I've never seen it since. It was bought by Father McGrath, an enthusiastic art collector who is presently living in Limerick."

All these paintings were stages towards achieving the fluency in oils to tackle the more complex figurative themes to which he found himself being drawn — but without departing from the flat look of his earlier work in acrylics.

He perfected a technique — used in the Downes portrait — which entails painting fairly accurately first but then softening the paint so that the brush strokes disappear. The difficulty was in achieving the right consistency of paint so that when softened it wouldn't oversoften and yet it wouldn't become too sticky either.

"I've always had this hatred of style. Other painters deliberately cultivate brush strokes to give character to their painting. I feel compelled to remove them.

"When I was doing *Liberty at the Barricades* and *The Third of May* I'd worry in case the black line I was using — purely to solve the problem of seeping paint — might develop into a gesture. I remember deliberately keeping the line at a constant half inch thickness throughout. I even made a little measure to check that

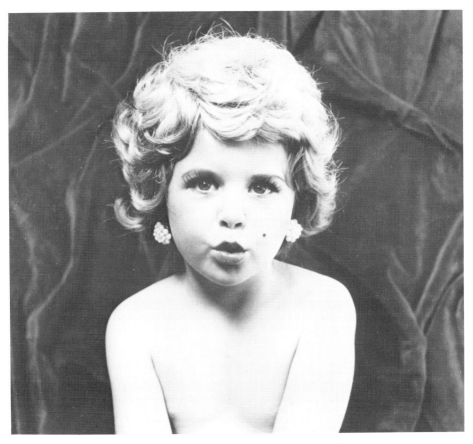

Juxtaposing roles. Six-year-old Rachel pretending to be Marilyn Monroe. One of the source photographs for the painting *Rachel/Marilyn*.

there was no deviation. I would have been horrified to have been identified with an artistic flourish."

Part of his disenchantment with Modernism was that it had degenerated into fashion. It had become too codified. If a painter was into any of the "isms" it became difficult for him to attempt anything else. He was typecast. He was the man who did the stripes or the blobs or the circles.

"Modernism turned into a form of academic art. I found it too narrow an area of expression.

"By working within the broader traditions of figurative painting I find I now have the freedom to do anything."

2

Betty was due to go into labour at any moment.
The telephone rang.
He grabbed the receiver.
"Yes?"

It was Ciaran Costello, projects manager for D.E. Williams, owners of the big 5-Star supermarket chain.

"I'd like to discuss a commission with you. How about lunch?"
"Sorry. I can't. Please phone back some other time."
"But this could be a very big commission for you."
"I can't talk about it now."
He put down the receiver.

Costello rang back. Ballagh kept putting him off without an explanation.
But he didn't give up.
They finally got together after Bruce was born.
"It's lucky for me he was so patient. The meeting turned out to be a watershed in my career."

Costello wanted an 80-foot mural for a supermarket in Clonmel. There was also a smaller commission for some paintings for the bar.

"This isn't De Medici patronage. It's business," he explained. Art was one of the most economical ways of covering a wall. They had commissioned a Cecil King tapestry for a project in Sligo. But a supermarket required a younger touch. Some kind of pop image.

"There wasn't anything airy-fairy about the commission," recalls Ballagh. "That appealed to me. People need to realise that using art is not something esoteric or unusual. That's still a bridge we must cross in Ireland."

The mural became a final summing-up of his people looking at paintings series. By turning Frank Stella's famous notched V's upside down he could make them join together to form a wave that seemed to go on forever. It was a visual pun on the repetition in abstract art.

He had to use material that would stand up to the rough and tumble of being in a public place. Mosaic was ruled out as being too expensive. He wouldn't have chosen it anyway. Formica was more to his liking. It could be washed down with soap and water. It wouldn't matter if children painted moustaches on it or used it for parking bicycles.

Portrait of Laurence Sterne. The idea of the subject materialising out of a daub of paint is prompted by the animated brush device in Walt Disney's *True Life* documentaries. Oil and acrylic on canvas, 58 x 144.

"Everyone thinks of Formica as plastic. But it's really a special type of impregnated paper. The parchment finish I selected is for all the world like water colour paper. It's without any shine, a crinkled, matte surface like the skin of an orange.

"You silkscreen your image on the paper sheets and they go into a press to be bound together with special brown paper sheets into a sheet of plastic by heat and pressure. In theory anything you can silkscreen can be reproduced in this plastic laminate."

But he pushed the technique beyond its normal use. Instead of solid colour he required fairly detailed figures. With the help of Donald Stewart, one of the designers at the Formica factory in Newcastle-upon-Tyne, he decided to enlarge photographs of figures to life-size so that the emulsion in the film literally became a dot: but the dot was organic rather than mechanical. The figures were then printed with the colours hand-painted, tinted like water colours. This meant that although each panel in the mural repeated several times, the colours of the clothes kept changing. Between trips to Newcastle, he tried to find a subject for the paintings in the bar. The contract specified a theme of local interest. He didn't know anything about Clonmel. Someone told him Laurence Sterne had been born there. He began reading *Tristram Shandy.* Although it had been written over two hundred years before he was born, the content and

The Life and Opinions of Tristram Shandy. Details from the Sterne novel are illustrated within the framework of the Hollywood device that depicts the elapse of time by flipping the pages of a book. Oil and acrylic on canvas, 60 x 432.

the humour struck an immediate chord. He put it down mesmerized. It was as if he had found in it a part of himself.

"It seems to me that he was waiting to meet Sterne and Sterne was waiting to meet him," says Kieran Hickey, who wrote a script with David Thompson in 1968 for a documentary film about Sterne — never produced — and gave Ballagh numerous leads in his research.

Sterne had ended up as a vicar in England and is often regarded as an English novelist. But all his formative years growing up were spent in Ireland. They conditioned the shape and tone of his writing.

Ballagh found parallels between this distancing and his own experience as a painter out of step with traditional concepts of national identity. He had worried about the occasional criticism that somehow his art was un-Irish. With Sterne he now found a worthy precedent:

> To write a book, is for the world like humming a song; — be but in tune with yourself . . . 'tis no matter how high or low you take it.

Irishness was not something to be imposed on art. You couldn't make a painting Irish by sticking on a little Celtic ornamentation or by evoking a rural idyll that passed away years before, if it ever existed at all.

"If you deal honestly with your own experience, as Sterne did and as I try to do, the Irishness will come out. It doesn't matter whether you're using Pop images or sharp-focus realism. You don't need any thatched cottages. Because you are Irish and because your

122

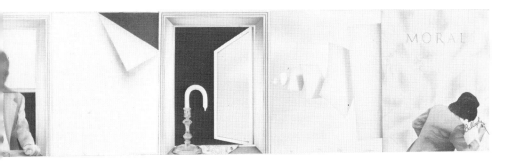

experience is Irish, the work will be Irish no matter what it's about."

Sterne had trained to draw before he ever wrote. His visual imagination shaped his whole approach to fiction. He didn't try to get inside his characters, as other novelists did, but deduced what they were from the meticulously observed detail of their outer lives. The surface of existence provided an inventory of their inner self.

"If ever a writer expressed the nature of writing and the consciousness of being a writer writing for an audience reading what one is writing, it was Sterne," says Hickey.

"If ever there was a painter who paints pictures about the consciousness of a painter as he paints pictures for an audience who are looking at a painting he has painted, it is Ballagh.

"Their work has this sense of a mutual awareness between the audience and the artist about being engaged in an act of creation."

Sterne provided Ballagh with the confidence to rediscover himself. He had worked his way through Modernism to a point at which he felt he was no longer a Modernist painter. He felt hamstrung by a philosophy which was holding him back from developing according to his own nature.

"I realised I'd been fudging my feelings and pretending they were not what they were in order to conform to the Modernist ethos. I'd been using literary devices and puns and all sorts of things that were taboo to Modernism but in a way that the paintings still looked Modernist and conformed to the tenets of Modernism."

To celebrate his liberation and to rejoice in the revelations of Sterne would require something bigger than the small canvas specified in the Clonmel commission.

Costello shared his enthusiasm. Two paintings were agreed: a 12 foot by 5 foot portrait of Sterne and a monumental 36 foot by 5 foot evocation of *Tristram Shandy* which would be one of the largest paintings of its kind undertaken in Ireland since Daniel Maclise, the nineteenth-century Cork narrative painter whose *Marriage of Strongbow and Aoife* dominates a hall in the National Gallery.

At Hickey's urging he went to London to see the Joshua Reynolds portrait of Sterne in the National Portrait Gallery. It had been taken down for cleaning. He explained to an attendant that he had come all the way from Dublin to see it.

"He took pity on me and allowed me down to the restoring room, leaving me alone with racks and racks of masterpieces. There was a colossal row afterwards. It was in the middle of the IRA bombings in 1975. And there was I, an unidentified Irishman, holding in my hands one of Britain's great national treasures!"

He wanted an image that would convey a sense of the apparent spontaneity of Sterne's style of writing ("Ask my pen. It governs me, I govern not it") while alluding humorously to the fact that he had been a painter.

"I'd been very much taken as a child by the way Walt Disney's *True Life* movies always started with a globe of the world revolving on its axis. An animated paint brush would then daub on, with a few quick brush strokes, trees and mountains and rivers, bringing to life a whole landscape.

"I always think a painting should look like that. It should never seem laboured. I think Sterne, like myself, was anything but spontaneous. But he gave the impression of spontaneity. That's the important thing."

Using the likeness from the Reynolds portrait, he depicted Sterne materialising in the wake of a hugely magnified paintbrush stroke.

He was still experimenting with oil and needed three preparatory sketches and a small study painting before he got the final image right.

"It was trial and error. Originally I painted it red. But I realised that it wouldn't do for someone who died of TB. In finally settling for green, which was aesthetically the right decision, I was also unconsciously making an ironic gesture to Irishness."

Sterne, spitting blood whenever he coughed, had an obsession about time. All his writing was an attempt to depict its passing with ever increasing exactitude.

To suggest this in *The Life and Opinions of Tristram Shandy* Ballagh again resorted to a movie image: the Hollywood convention of illustrating an elapse of time by flipping the pages of a book.

The painting took the format of a strip of pages from the novel which appear to be blowing away like leaves in the wind of time. Tristram is shown in surreal close-up, his head a drooping clockface, about to be guillotined by a window, a reference to his mother's untimely remark ("Pray, my Dear, quoth my mother, have you not forgot to wind up the clock?") which condemned him to a life of misfortune. Ballagh also works in an allusion to an unfortunate incident when, as a child wanting to pee in a hurry, he had gone to an open window, forgetting that his uncle had removed the sash weight to make a toy cannon. This same uncle Toby, on being asked once where he had been wounded during his war years, replied that there were two answers, "Outside the walls of Namur" or "In the groin". Ballagh frames each of these images in a window, in keeping with Sterne's speculation on the consequences of there being a window in every human breast through which could be seen the soul. The final 'page' in the sequence, entitled 'Moral', shows Ballagh bending down to sign the corner, a mocking reference to his gesture in the last of his pictures of people looking at paintings. Having signed off Modernism, he was now signing on as a figurative painter.

3

He completed the Clonmel commissions in 1976 only to find himself on the dole again. There were legal difficulties over the final payment. D.E. Williams paid promptly, but the other company involved in the project were reluctant to pay the £3,000 owed to him.

Some idea of the difficulties in earning a living wage from art in Ireland in the 1970s is revealed in his reply to questions about his future plans, which he made in the course of an unsuccessful application for an art fellowship.

"If I am so successful, as everyone reminds me, how is it that I am still broke," he asked with rhetorical irony. "If I have managed to sell practically everything that I made, how is it that I still have no money?

"I've consulted an accountant, Mr X, who states bluntly that my present position is practically untenable. He cites a simple example, based on the sale of a painting, retailing at £100, which had taken one week to complete. The following deductions have to be made:

Dealer's commission	£33.00
10% VAT on dealer's commission	£ 3.33
Framing	£10.00
Material	£15.00
20% VAT on material	£ 3.00
Studio rent, heat, light	£ 5.00
Miscellaneous, photography, etc.	£ 5.67
	Total £75.00

This leaves the artist with £25.00, not much for a week's work!

"Mr X suggests either an increase in price or in output. I discard his first suggestion as being inapplicable in the present economic situation. And even if increased productivity were a possibility, which I doubt as I already work a 7-hour, 6-day week, I don't think there are sufficient Irish buyers to absorb a yearly output of 50 paintings from one artist. The costings for exhibiting abroad are even less favourable than those for Ireland. Transportation costs are enormous and foreign dealers take 50%. I have learned to my detriment that exhibitions abroad are good for the ego, bad for the pocket."

The application failed, but the Arts Council came to his rescue by commissioning a portrait of Sheridan Le Fanu, who had lived at 70 Merrion Square in the building they now used for their offices.

Only a few months before he had been in Brussels talking about Le Fanu with Scutinaire. The coincidence appealed to him: it was the sort of thing that might happen in a Le Fanu story.

Finding a likeness to work from proved unexpectedly difficult. Le Fanu was an inward-looking and reclusive person: not at all the sort to pose for a portrait or a camera. Des Hickey, Kieran's author brother who had published a book on Le Fanu's horror stories, helped him track down a photo taken in the garden at Merrion Square. But it was too blurred to work from. A portrait by Brinsley Le Fanu, the son, in the National Gallery wasn't much better, although the relative who donated the picture to the gallery, referred to it, in a letter of provenance on the gallery's files, as being "a great likeness of how I remembered him as a child". Eventually Ballagh worked from a small etching of this painting.

Le Fanu is generally regarded as one of the first of the psychological novelists. All his stories play on the imagination to stir unconscious fears. The horror is in the reader's own mind.

Ballagh evokes this concept of an interior landscape with an ingenious adaptation of Sterne's idea of the window as a peephole to the soul. Le Fanu stands at a Georgian window holding a candle — a reference to the fact that he always wrote at night, keeping awake with copious draughts of green tea — but the window is in fact part of him and through its small opening we see within him a ruined house isolated beneath a high empty sky.

Apparently during Le Fanu's last illness he had a recurring dream about being an old house falling down. When he finally died the doctor announced to his assembled family that "the house had finally fallen".

Ballagh painted the sky in the manner of Caspar David Friedrich, a nineteenth-century artist noted for strange romantic landscapes very much in the eerie spirit of Le Fanu.

"It doesn't matter if people don't make all these connections. The point is that they help me make the picture. A painting is like a cake with layers and layers, all of which contribute to the taste of the cake."

In painting Sterne and Le Fanu he was essentially exploring the creative process in others: he was an outsider looking in. Logic now led him to probe his own experience as a creative artist.

One by one the taboos of Modernism were being shed. First with the literary allusions: paintings that drew their meaning from beyond the actual framework of the canvas. And now he took a step even further away from pure formalism, moving into the area of autobiographical art with a study of his own studio.

"It might not seem such an amazing thing to do. But I was entering for the first time directly into my own personal environment."

My Studio 1969 is a painting within a painting. On a desk in front of *Liberty at the Barricades* he has assembled the tools of his trade: a roll of masking tape, brushes, paints, a rubber, a brochure for acrylic paints, a copy of the *Irish Independent* with the headline RIOTS IN DERRY and a reproduction of Delacroix's Liberty.

In a sense the painting is a cheat. His studio wasn't at Parliament Street in 1969. He used at that time a room belonging to Bill Murphy, the designer, over his parents' flat at Elgin Road. *Liberty at*

Hollywood quotation. A Gordon Lambert screen becomes the medium for a joke on the cliche Mae West bedroom scene. Acrylic and oil on our canvas panels, 60 x 18.

the Barricades took up an entire wall and he could only step back a couple of feet to look at it. He didn't see it properly until it was eventually hung in the gallery.

One idea led to another. *Studio with Modigliani Print* shows an easel with a drawing of the painting we are looking at and on the easel within the drawing there is in turn a blank canvas. The reference to Modigliani is sly: a previous owner of the studio had left a Modigliani postcard pinned on the wall.

He no longer felt obliged to sublimate his natural instinct to make jokes in paintings. It hadn't been the done thing for a Modernist to be humorous. Puns were regarded as essentially literary devices and therefore suspect.

A typically offbeat idea of Gordon Lambert provided the stimulus to rid himself finally of any such inhibition. Lambert had found an old screen in the family attic. He suggested that Ballagh should attempt to convert it into an art work.

"My only experience of such a screen was in the old cowboy movies when the heroine would invariably undress behind a screen while talking with the hero."

Which prompted the idea of a double-sided painting. From in front you see lingerie draped casually over the top of the screen. Go around the other side and you find a nude painting of a girl — his first of Betty — languidly preparing her toilet.

The flamboyant Nicholas Treadwell meanwhile commissioned a work for an exhibition on the theme of "Bottoms" which provided an opportunity for more humour. His response was a rear view of a male nude admiring Goya's celebrated portrait of the Duchess of Alba clothed.

Emboldened by these successes he entered a work for the International Exhibition of Humour and Satire in Bulgaria and won a top prize with a painting of a flasher in a dirty mack revealing all to a disdainful Mona Lisa. He repeated this achievement two years later with a joke version of a typical equestrian work by Stubbs in which a gallery attendant is shown sweeping away horse droppings from beneath the painting. Both these works are now on permanent exhibition at the House of Humour and Satire, Gabravo, Bulgaria.

Since currency could not be taken out of Bulgaria, he and Betty travelled there to collect and spend the prize money.

On arrival in Sofia they were directed to the imposing Artists Union building.

"Ah, Mr Ballagh, but you are married!" exclaimed an official.

"Yes," he replied apprehensively, afraid for a moment that in some way this might be a disqualification.

"In that case you are entitled to additional money," he was told.

A possible explanation for Mona Lisa's smile, as revealed at the International Exhibition of Humour and Satire, Bucharest. Oil and acrylic on canvas, 38 x 24.

"Do you have children?"

"Yes. A girl and a boy."

"That also entitles you to an extra allowance."

Ballagh began to regret that he hadn't given himself a more typically Irish family.

"Sofia is a café society like Paris except that the cafés were all State-owned. There are no advertisements, only billboards everywhere exhorting you to work harder for the Revolution.

"We stayed in the best hotel living on champagne and caviar to the accompaniment of an old-style orchestra of the kind found in the Grand Hotels at the turn of the century. You had this sense of being separate from everyone around you, parasites in a proletarian promised land.

"It brought home to me the irony implicit in criticisms of the Communist world. Here was a society in which law and order ruled supreme. No hooliganism. No vandalism. No muggings. The streets were clean. No pop music blaring from the shops. No sex shops. Everyone worked dutifully. Strikes were unknown. In many ways it corresponded to a Tory dream world!"

But he was impressed by the way in which artists were automatically integrated into society, their material needs guaranteed and protected the same as any other worker's.

"I came away more than ever convinced of the need for artists to be organised."

4

The Mona Lisa flasher could be acclaimed behind the supposedly strait-laced Iron Curtain — but a variation proved too much for Kilkenny Arts Week in 1978.

Barrie Cooke, in the course of organising an exhibition of kites from Thailand, Malaya, Japan and Korea, where kites have been both an art and a sport for a long time, solicited works in the medium from a number of Irish artists, including Ballagh.

"There is almost no limit as to what a painter or a sculptor might do once his imagination were hit by the idea of a kite," he told them. He particularly asked Ballagh to make a figurative kite.

All the images of figures with capes that first came to mind were in the Superman and Batman style. Ballagh dismissed them as being too corny. The idea of the flasher seemed an obvious and practical choice.

"I'm not so naive that I didn't think the subject might be controversial. So I deliberately adopted a very stylised and non-realistic treatment that I thought wouldn't cause offence."

A month before the festival he sent photographs of his proposal to the organising committee. Preliminary sketches were shown at the David Hendriks gallery, one of which was bought by the Arts Council.

But hours before the official opening of the festival, the chairman, the Rev. Brian Harvey, acting on behalf of the committee, removed Ballagh's kite on the grounds that "its display under the circumstances would be inappropriate".

Cooke immediately denounced the action as censorship. Theo McNabb, one of Ballagh's closest friends, withdrew his own work in protest. "I don't see how anyone could have taken offence," he complained. He was joined by Camille Souter, who wrote to the *Irish Times:* "It is not possible to paint if there is any dictatorship of what should or should not be painted." Michael Farrell sent a

The kite that never flew. The flasher image suppressed by the Kilkenny Arts Week committee.

telegram from Paris demanding that his work be withdrawn — but this was ignored by the Festival committee.

Overnight Ballagh's kite became an all too typically Irish *cause célébrè,* prompting the customary amused headlines in the British tabloids. FLASH OF INSPIRATION DOESN'T GET A CHANCE, joked the *Daily Mail.* Cartoonist Bob Fannin in the *EveningHerald,* depicted two girls ignoring a flasher in St Stephen's Green with the deprecating comment: "Definitely not an original Ballagh!" Hugh Leonard quipped in his *Sunday Independent* column

"Definitely not an original Ballagh." Bob Fannin's cartoon comment on the kite controversy, published in the Evening Herald.

that they were "the most public private parts in Ireland". Colm Ó Briain formally demanded an explanation from the committee "so that the matter may be considered by the Arts Council". There was an absurd sequel when police caused newsagents to withdraw copies of *Grapevine* magazine, which had reproduced the kite on its cover, following complaints from the *Parents Concern* lobby.

"My only real regret is that I never got a chance to fly it. It was eventually returned to the Hendriks gallery damaged beyond repair."

Purchased by the Arts Council, the sketch now, ironically, hangs in Butler House in Kilkenny.

"Perhaps it was some kind of turning point in censorship. But somehow you always get into these kind of rows over works that are not all that important. The battleground is never of your own choosing."

The fact that the same image could be freely shown in a gallery but not on a magazine cover or at a public festival epitomised the double standard of morality prevalent in Ireland. What was forbidden to ordinary people was readily permitted for a cultural and social élite. It was not what an artist painted that bothered the establishment but to whom it was shown.

Two years earlier Dublin Corporation had invoked an obscure bye-law to suppress a work he proposed to exhibit at the first Oasis show of outdoor sculpture in Merrion Square.

"My idea was to erect a 12 foot high pyramid of barbed wire — about 500 bales in all — as a comment on internment in the North.

"Ruari Quinn, then a Labour Councillor, fought hard but the Corporation legal department stood firm on an old bye-law stating that there could be no barbed wire on Corporation property."

It would have been one of his few directly political statements since splashing blood on the floor of Project for the 1972 Living Art.

Politics in the North had been pushed aside by the mounting Provo campaign of indiscriminate bombing and murder of civilians and members of the Royal Ulster Constabulary. Internment divided the community along traditional sectarian lines. The Peace Movement — unlike the Sabine Women in the David painting — had failed to interpose itself between the warring factions in the internecine struggle. The British Government's inability to impose further reforms on the loyalist majority — manifested by the wrecking of the power-sharing experiment as a result of the 1974 Protestant workers' strike — scuttled the possibility of any peaceful or non-sectarian Civil Rights movement. Ballagh's youthful hope for a 32-county socialist republic seemed more and more a pipedream as the familiar tribal shibboleths drowned out all other voices. There was no longer a clear option with which he could identify beyond his natural abhorrence of the mindless blood-letting.

This growing lack of personal identification was already evident in *Winchester 73,* ostensibly relating to the hunger strike in that year by the Price sisters, who had been convicted of exploding car-bombs in London, but in fact a Pop-style comment — emphasised by the appalling pun in the title — on media perception of the North.

"It struck me that when certain people suddenly spring into notoriety, the only images we have of them tend to be police photographs. The media then transmits these around the world. I wanted to focus on the impersonality of these images by painting them without comment exactly as they appeared in the newspapers — in this case a composite row of mug shots of the Price sisters and

Miami Murders. A screenprinted photograph of the ambushed pop musicians, the broken glass again a reference to violent death.

their co-defendants in the Winchester bomb trial."

The monochrome image is as bland as any Warhol Campbells soup can. It is apolitical, neither supporting nor rejecting the action of the sisters, although, as Brian Trench points out, the choice of subject suggests some degree of involvement.

The shift in direction of his career towards Europe — thirteen exhibitions there in two years — had distanced him further from the North.

But nobody in Ireland can for long look away from the carnage that has become an everyday reality there: there is always some new outrage to make it part of their own experience.

Late in 1975 Loyalist extremists ambushed the Miami Showband, one of the Republic's most popular groups, on their way from a gig in the North. The musicians were ordered out of their van and shot in cold blood at the roadside. One of the dead was lead singer Fran O'Toole.

Ballagh knew the hall where they had played. He had many times travelled the same route with the Chessmen. He had played once with O'Toole.

Over the months that followed he tried to distill an image that would externalise his personal shock. The Miami management were initially reluctant to collaborate by providing him with a photograph of the band. They were wary of attempts to exploit the atrocity.

His idea was to screen the band's picture in red on a glass mirror and then shatter it with a bullet. The mirror would be set in a fibre glass resin to freeze the pieces on impact. But a real bullet failed to produce the required effect. It went right through the glass and left a clean hole. Eventually he succeeded with a metal punch which shattered the glass in a way that satisfied him.

Shattered glass had been a symbol of death in the Connolly ikon. But since the glass was now a mirror, the viewer this time was also looking at a shattered image of his own face.

The print, which he exhibited at the Tokyo Biennale in 1976, was limited to five copies, the minimum necessary to recoup his costs.

"It was a purely personal statement. I was concerned that no profit should accrue from it. The danger in any political art is that it inadvertently takes advantage of other people's tragedy."

5

The continuing preoccupation with mirrors and windows led him, perhaps inevitably for a Dubliner, to Flann O'Brien's *The Third Policeman.*

"The whole book is about repetitive and recessive imagery. Doors within doors, rooms within rooms. You're never sure where you are. Essentially it's a game about guilt, the punishment for which is an eternity of the same. You look in windows and you see yourself looking out."

The six paintings with which he interpreted this theme were the first inspired by a literary theme not to have been commissioned. The personal identification is emphasised by the photograph on the catalogue cover, a reflected self-portrait on glass in which he looks out from behind bars, the effect of the reflection being to make his prison everyone's prison. *The Barracks* places the door of a garda

Day for Night. De Selby's idea that night is merely dirt: wipe it away and daylight reappears. From *The Third Policeman* series. Acrylic and oil on canvas, 30 x 24.

station incongruously in an empty landscape, a mirror inside further challenging conventional notions of space. *Day for Night* toys with a theory propounded by De Selby, the imaginary philosopher invented by Flann O'Brien, that night is merely an accretion of dirt and pollution: wash it clean and daylight returns.

He initially planned about a dozen paintings in the series which would form a circular environment in the gallery, in keeping with the cyclical nature of the book, which begins and ends with the same words. "But that would have been too much of a fairground show. I began to worry that I was getting away from what painting was about."

Although he had lost faith in Modernism, he was still using Modernist tricks. There had been no essential formal change to accompany the move towards literary content. He was still painting within the Modernist ethos, like a lapsed Catholic who hasn't stopped going to Mass.

No 3 was the final break, an autobiographical portrait of himself

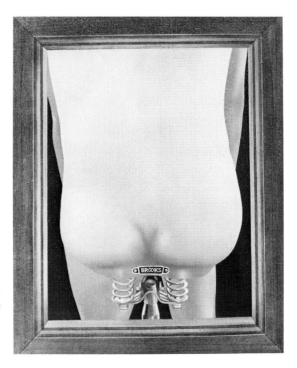

The Atomic Theory. The bicycle as an extension of the body. From *The Third Policeman* series. Acrylic and oil on canvas, 30 x 24.

with his family posing in front of their terraced home at 3 Temple Cottages which he painted entirely within the traditional framework of geometric perspective as laid down since the Renaissance.

"It took a bit of soul searching. I knew I'd be branded as a conservative and a reactionary. But once I painted it I realised that this was the direction my work would take for the foreseeable future. Modernism was something I was able to work through and come out the other side.

"All I was doing now was articulating a picture in terms of a commonly received language. Philosophically it was no more real than any of my other paintings or any abstract painting. The difference was in how people perceived it. They had been conditioned for 500 years to see in a way I was now painting. They could see fluently in this language just as they could speak fluently in English. I was simply choosing to communicate to them in their own language."

As a joke he hid his face behind an open book with the title *How to*

Make Art Commercial. It was an ironic comment on the fact that although he had achieved something of a reputation as a painter, he was still on and off the dole. He wanted to emphasise that art is just another job and that artists share the same mundane problems as anyone else.

"What do you do for a living?" someone once asked him.

"I'm an artist."

"A commercial artist or a real artist?"

"I would hope that I'm a commercial artist in the sense that people want my work and are prepared to buy it," he replied.

He doesn't see anything disreputable in admitting that he earns his living by selling his art. Nor does he see anything degrading in being a popular painter. "If you're involved in communication, the logic is to communicate to the greatest number of people."

He now felt an enormous sense of relief. He no longer needed to hold back his instincts while painting. He had found his natural voice.

He took advantage of every trip abroad to visit the great museums to see work by the old masters. Five years before he would have spent all his time in the modern art galleries.

"I identified especially with the fifteenth-century Flemish painters. I loved the meticulous precision of Jan Van Eyck, the greedy eye for detail."

There was a sense in them of cold Northern skies, of interior worlds closely observed: the claustrophobic experience that had stimulated the obsessive detail of Celtic illuminated manuscripts.

Ballagh relates Ireland's visual heritage to this Northern tradition in European painting, which possesses quite distinct qualities to those obtaining in Mediterranean countries. As Michelangelo is reputed to have remarked: "In Flanders they paint with a view to external exactness . . . " The world around the painter rather than an imagined world is recorded with meticulous care. Man is shown as he is without any of the mystifying aura of an Italian or Greek demi-god. "The North was dark and cold and damp — no place for frescoes," argues Michael Levy in his book *From Giotto to Cezanne.* "It is as if lack of light and space had constricted the painters: endless intricate detail serves in place of larger harmonies". This Northern coolness is evident not only in the work of Vermeer and the Dutch masters, but in Casper David Friedrich and in the Pre-Raphaelites in the nineteenth century, and more recently in the

German New Sachlichkeit, a group of painters who "captured the face of their time in many nuances, soberly and unsentimentally, with sympathy but without illusions, and above all clearly." It begins, according to Wieland Schmid, with the banal everyday objects which surround us but aims at a reinterpretation of the world.

These are the roots Ballagh has eventually come to recognise in his own painting. But to feel an affinity with the past is not necessarily to turn back the clock. The cult of newness for the sake of newness has been one of the fallacies of Modernism. Which is why Ballagh likes to quote Jean Luc Godard: "There is no progress in art . . . only change."

Many people regard *No 3* as a going back. "But I saw myself as reconnecting with a tradition that never died and that continued, even while Modernism was rampant, with painters like Balthus, Stanley Spencer, Edward Hopper and Andrew Wyeth."

All of this experience is consolidated in pictorial terms in *The Conversation,* which is derived from Vermeer's *The Artist in His Studio* and shows Ballagh himself, glimpsed through a doorway, talking with Vermeer. The Dutch master, elbow on a book entitled *Modern Art,* is obviously in argumentative mood. A mirror on the wall facing him reflects nothing, suggesting that Ballagh has conjured up his ghost. Outside the room there is a blank space on a wall where one of Ballagh's earlier paintings, presumably Modernist, has been taken down.

"Literally and physically I'm connecting myself with a tradition that has existed for hundreds of years. But I'm not going back to Vermeer, he's coming forward to my period."

Ballagh is attempting to see with Vermeer's eyes but in the light of all that has happened to art and society in the years in between.

No 3 was exhibited at the David Hendriks Gallery in 1977. Afterwards Philip MacDermott called to his studio. In partnership with David Marcus at the Poolbeg Press he had been a major force in breaking the cultural dominance of London publishers by providing a cheap local paperback outlet for new Irish fiction.

Ballagh half expected to be invited to design book covers. That did come later. But after a wide-ranging conversation lasting several hours he found himself with a commission to paint a portrait of James Plunkett, whose short stories had been published by Poolbeg. MacDermott felt that there were far too few portraits of living Irish writers. He had been impressed by the way *No 3* represented people in terms of their environment. He thought it would be intriguing to see how this approach would work in portrait.

"I never considered myself a portrait painter in the traditional sense and I still don't. But the whole idea of doing commissioned portraits appealed to me. It was a reinforcing of the way I was beginning to feel about art.

"It seemed to me that it was harmful for the artist to aspire to the special role he had in the Modernist era. He should be more like the artist in the Renaissance or in sixteenth-century Holland, somebody who did a job like everybody else. Commissions were a part of all that. They made the artist an attached person."

6

Plunkett sits writing in longhand on a clipboard at an old-style wooden desk. Behind him on the wall hangs a viola and a framed photograph of the famous shot of James Larkin, arms outspread, urging on workers during the 1913 lockout in Dublin, a reference to Plunkett's trade union background and to *Strumpet City,* the epic novel in which he immortalised the working-class Dublin of that period. Several of his published works are piled on the desk. A sheet of viola music — a Beethoven string quartet — tips over the edge. The floor is tiled. The colours are predominantly brown and ochre.

He had met Plunkett over lunch and taken several rolls of film of him in his home. He found him very modest about his achievements, not at all out-going: nearer to Le Fanu than Sterne. The austerity of the tiled room is intended to convey this. The real floor is in fact carpeted. But tiles seemed to go better with the longhand and the wooden desk, suggesting the aura of a schoolroom.

The tiles are derived from illustrations in a Victorian catalogue belonging to Stephen Pearce, the potter.

"I'd been longing for a chance to use them. Gorgeous brown and ochre patterns which seemed to suit Plunkett. People unconsciously have colour schemes for themselves. I certainly tend to think of them in terms of their colours. Jim always seemed to be in browns and greens. This set the tone for the portrait."

Ballagh is himself a walking illustration of this theory. He invariably wears blues and whites. Perhaps because he has blue eyes. He has never attempted to rationalise it.

Portrait of James Plunkett. A visual inventory of the author's
life: his books and his music. Acrylic and oil on canvas, 60 x 48.

"People have told me it's an affectation to wear white shoes. But I've worn them since my showbusiness days. And on a purely practical level, it means you tend to get stood on less in a crowd!

"I make very few choices about my clothes. Just a batch of the same jeans and shirts again every time. I didn't wear ties for years. But then I realised, like Warhol, that there was nothing more bourgeois than being afraid to appear bourgeois."

He discovered that Plunkett was an accomplished musician. He and his wife played string quartets at weekends with John Beckett. So he introduced the viola in the background. To ensure that nobody confused it with a violin — because of the scale of the painting — he slipped in the sheet of music (some critics still managed to get it wrong).

The offers of further commissions that followed the Plunkett portrait provided a way out of his economic difficulties, a chance to buy time to pursue his other more personal works without the pressure to make a living from them. But the commissions were not to him a lesser form of painting because of that. As with all his work, they became a challenge in problem-solving, an opportunity to expand his vocabulary.

Staff from the Olympia Theatre had collected money for a portrait of Brendan Smith to commemorate his achievement in keeping the theatre open after the ceiling collapsed during a rehearsal for a Noel Pearson production of *West Side Story*. Michael Scott, as Chairman of the Dublin Theatre Festival which Smith directed, suggested that they approach Ballagh.

The funds available were limited. This dictated that the painting would need to be completed relatively quickly: time for an artist is money. Instead of painting Smith's familiar suit in detail, as he

No. 53 Winter in Ronda. An autobiographical variation on Velasquez's *Las Meninas.* The Ballagh family on holiday in Spain. ACrylic and oil on canvas, 72 x 96.

No. 3. A self-portrait with Betty and the children outside their home at Temple Cottages. Oil and acrylic on canvas, 72 x 96.

Portrait of Brendan Smith, paid for by the staff of the Olympia
Theatre, where it now hangs. Oil on canvas, 60 x 60.

might normally have done, he simply delineated it with pinstripe
patterns. But the stylised composition resulting from the economy
of means in fact evoked an appropriate theatricality. Without
knowing him, one would instantly identify Smith as a stage
personality. Yet this effect is achieved without caricature.

The stimulus of meeting a deadline is part of the appeal of
commissioned work. It conforms with Ballagh's desire to have a
specific role in society. A last-minute approach from an architect
friend, Declan Grehan, to produce a painting within ten days to
celebrate the opening of the huge new Platin cement works at

Drogheda was accordingly too intriguing to refuse.

"One of the things that I enjoy about jobs like that is that they oblige me to look closely at areas of experience that I might not otherwise notice. The Platin works is out of this world, one of the largest of its kind ever built. The cooling tower is taller than Liberty Hall. The kilns that make the cement are big revolving drums that heat to thousands of degrees. It all seemed to me like Cape Canaveral. So I depicted it in that way, looming over the horizon like something out of science fiction, the quarry pool in the foreground reflecting a purple Casper Friedrich sky."

That autumn Gordon Lambert telephoned in the middle of the night from Wexford Opera Festival, full of enthusiasm for Bernadette Greevy's singing in the title role of *Herodiade*. Here was an Irish artist who had reached an international standard of

Dawn at Platin. A futuristic impression of the Drogheda cement works, commissioned by Irish Cement Ltd. for presentation to the Minister for Transport and Power. Acrylic and oil on canvas, 36 x 24.

The completed Downes portrait oil on canvas, 48 x 60.

performance: he felt that her achievement should be marked in the form of a portrait.

"Portraiture in Ireland was too preoccupied with the dead," he recalls. "I wanted a young Irish artist to paint another young Irish artist."

Grand opera was not a form of music Ballagh could readily relate to. But this didn't matter. He was attracted to Greevy as someone totally dedicated to her craft.

"She keeps polishing it, perfecting it, honing her voice as an instrument. I could respond to that. As professionals we were kindred spirits."

He took countless photographs of her standing beside her piano and even did a preparatory sketch in that manner.

Inside No. 3 After Modernisation. The variety of styles, from Cubism to Art Deco, is a rejection of the domination of art by any one "ism". Acrylic and oil on canvas, 84 x 60.

A second Bernadette Greevy portrait, commissioned by her husband, the late Peter Tattan, showing her at home with Peter and their son Hugh. Oil on canvas, 24 x 18.

"But it didn't suggest anything special about her. She could have been a Lord Mayor's wife posing in the parlour."

Cataloguing her career in his mind led him to a *trompe l'oeil* image, stylistically very much in keeping with the style of opera in its heyday in the last century: he drew back a curtain theatrically on a cabinet of shelves arranged with programmes of some of her international performances (at the Proms in the Albert Hall, with the Halle Orchestra, at Covent Garden and the Edinburgh Festival), cassettes of her recordings, a bust of Beethoven, a manuscript sheet of her favourite song *Chanson Triste* by Henri Duparc, books on Mahler, Berlioz, Fauré, Elgar and Massenet, composers with whom she had a particular affinity, a plugged-in recorder and stereo loudspeakers. Her likeness is not shown directly but in three different publicity formats: a framed colour photograph, a black and white shot on the sleeve of a record, a small profile on a cassette.

As a gesture to Lambert's fascination with kinetic art, the portrait is wired to a looped tape of Bernadette singing Brahms, the music being triggered off whenever anyone moves into range.

Bernadette's pleasure in the result was qualified by one regret. "It's lovely to have your portrait painted by Robert but terrible not to be able to keep it," she told me.

As a surprise for her birthday, her husband Peter Tattan commissioned a second, more intimate portrait.

"I began telling Robert which way I wanted it but he pulled me up short, saying he'd do it his way, that was his job. I'm glad he did."

Ballagh painted her more softly the second time and in a domestic setting to contrast with her public image, showing her holding a photograph of Peter and their son Hugh.

"It's light-hearted and affectionate," she told me. "He has a great sense of humour but none of this talking in riddles."

7

Ballagh had received surprisingly few Irish grants or awards: the Carroll's Prize at the Living Art in 1969, the Douglas Hyde Prize for his Connolly picture and the Alice Berger Hammerschlag Award, which financed his first trip to the United States in 1971. Otherwise his income from art was entirely dependent on sales and commissions. Which made the £3,000 Gainey Award from the Irish-American Cultural Institute in 1978 all the more welcome.

"Its purpose is to stimulate creative output," Dr Eoin McKiernan told him. But its immediate effect was to make possible an ambition to spend part of the winter in Spain with Betty and the children.

On the way south to Ronda, which is in the province of Malaga, where they had the loan of a cottage, they stopped over in Madrid to visit the Prado, seeing for the first time the paintings of Goya and Velazquez he had pored over in reproduction.

The sheer scale of Velazquez's *Las Meninas,* for long one of his favourites, was overwhelming, coming upon it in its high-ceilinged room, cordoned off from the public, its huge black frame over 12 foot high.

"On the surface it looks a fairly simple idea, a painting within a painting in which Velazquez is seen behind his easel, doing a portrait

Inside No. 3. Defying conventional visual logic with several vanishing points. Autobiographical painting inspired by Duchamp's *Abstracted Nude Descending Staircase.* Oil and acrylic on canvas, 72 x 72.

of the King and Queen of Spain. But the more you look the more you become aware of many complex and subtle layers of meaning, not the least being that it's one of the few self-portraits of Velazquez."

He had brought all his painting equipment with him and dutifully started sketching and painting watercolours once he arrived in Ronda.

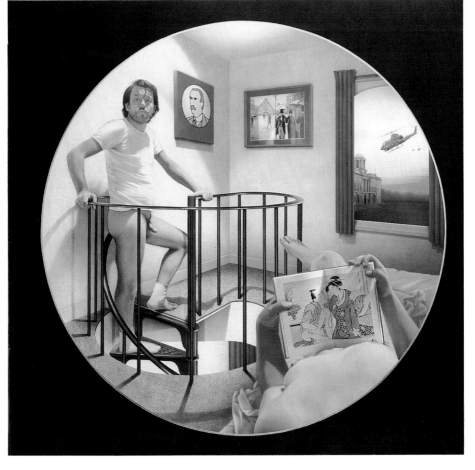

Upstairs No. 3. Reversal of roles in *Inside No. 3.* A commentary
on attitudes to the nude in Western and Eastern art. Acrylic and
oil on canvas, 72 x 96.

"But I soon realised I was being ridiculous. That wasn't the sort of
artist I was."

Instead he used the experience as a sabbatical to rethink some of
his ideas. Re-reading *Ulysses* helped to clarify the whole concept of
being an artist and being Irish.

"Joyce succeeded in making a statement of universal significance by dealing honestly with his own experience and by concentrating on things he knew intimately."

One quote in particular appealed to Ballagh, so much so that he noted it down and later used it as a motto for his book of photographs of Dublin:

> For myself, I always write about Dublin, because if I can get to the heart of Dublin I can get to the heart of all the great cities of the world. In the particular is found the universal.

Back in his studio he sought to get down on canvas images that might resolve the thoughts and feelings stimulated by being in Spain. The starting point inevitably was *Las Meninas* but, unlike his homage to Goya in *The Third of May,* in which he has simply transcribed the composition into contemporary language, he now did the reverse, changing the structure of the picture while adhering to the traditional language of geometric perspective in which it had been painted.

The theme, appropriately, was a holiday snapshot of his family assembled — in a variation of *No 3* — outside the sundrenched cottage in Ronda.

Unlike Velazquez, who placed himself behind an easel, Ballagh

A photograph of Number 53, a cottage near Ronda, owned by Harry Thubron, an English artist, and his wife Elma, where the Ballagh family stayed in 1978.

sits on a chair in the shade, reading an art book with a reproduction of *Les Meninas* on the cover. A pile of books, including *Ulysses,* are on the ground beside him. Through the open door the mirror, which in Velazquez's painting provided a glimpse of the king and queen, now reflects Ballagh himself photographing the scene. Rachel, his daughter, in a bikini, echoes the pose of the little princess. Bruce pokes at a lizard with a stick instead of teasing a dog as the dwarf did in the original picture.

This is the first painting in which Ballagh used oil glazes for shadows, capturing a sense of the brilliant light of Spain with lovely blue tones which cause the figures to jump out of the picture.

His distinctive approach to portraiture, allowing subjects to reveal themselves, like Sterne's fictional characters, through the surface detail of their lives, was now beginning to attract more commissions than he could immediately tackle.

The challenge in each case was to find the detail that would open what Sterne had called "the window in the breast". With Hugh Leonard it was the golden era of Hollywood. Whenever they met at parties they invariably talked about old movies. Both had spent the best part of their childhood in cinemas: the experience probably conditioned Leonard's vision as a playwright as much as it had his own as a painter.

This prompted a portrait in the monochrome tones of the silver screen: particularly apt since Leonard so often dressed in grey anyway. The scale of the canvas conforms to the old academy $1\frac{1}{3}:1$ screen ratio and the pose recalls countless shots of Sam Spade alone in his office at night, the lights of the city glimpsed through the window. But behind Leonard is a view of Dalkey Island by moonlight: he has his back to an image from his own childhood.

The page of manuscript in the electric typewriter on the desk in the foreground is in the format of a movie script: "Author sits cigar in hand facing artist sitting in author's chair". Ballagh borrowed a Douglas Sirk screenplay for *Captain Lightfoot* from Kieran Hickey to get the cinematic jargon right.

The picture is cropped like a frame from a movie — a medium shot — with part of the typewriter offscreen. It simulates the depth of field camera style made popular by *Citizen Kane:* those were the days when producers insisted, "We paid for the goddam set, let's see all of it."

Leonard's appreciation of the portrait is indicated by its pride of

Highfield (originally titled *The Pause That Refreshes*). The setting is the artist's cottage in Cork. Oil on canvas, 73 x 73.

Portrait of Noel Browne. The cruciform format makes ironic comment on the Socialist politician's lifelong struggle against clerical interference in Irish political life. Oil on canvas, 72 x 54.

place in the hall of his flat in Dalkey. He regards it as a new genre of "statement" portraiture.

"I was afraid he might have been disappointed because I hadn't used colour. But he understood immediately what I was trying to do."

Philip MacDermott followed up the Plunkett portrait with a commission to design all six covers for the Poolbeg spring list in 1979: it offered the chance to disseminate art images to a much larger audience than Ballagh ever reached through the existing gallery/museum system.

"One of the perverse things about Modernism was that it turned its back on the public, choosing art for art's sake, which in essence meant an élitist audience, at the very time when it had become possible through reproduction to reach the broadest, largest and most aesthetically aware audience any artist could ever desire."

The concept of what is or is not art is not some timeless absolute, fixed and unchanging. It has varied through history in response to shifting historical and technological circumstances.

"At one stage, the original art work was part of the place where it was to be seen," Ballagh pointed out in a lecture at the Douglas Hyde gallery in 1981. "Frescoes and mosaics were an integral fixture in the building for which they were designed."

But this status quo, imposed by the Renaissance popes and princes, was disrupted by the advent of capitalism. Karl Marx was the first to draw attention to the way in which such changes effect changes in man's consciousness.

"Constant revolutionising of production, uninterrupted disturbance of all social conditions, everlasting uncertainty and agitation distinguish the bourgeois epoch from all earlier ones," he wrote in *The Communist Manifesto.*

"All fixed, fast-frozen relations with their train of ancient and venerable prejudices and opinions are swept away, all new formed ones become antiquated before they can ossify . . . the need of a constantly expanding market for its products chase the bourgeoisie over the whole surface of the globe. It must nestle everywhere, settle everywhere, establish connections everywhere."

This new mobile social order led to a gradual replacing of the fixed fresco and then the mosaic by the portable oil painting on canvas.

"Art became objectified," argues Ballagh, "and like all personal possessions, could be packed up and taken where required. This

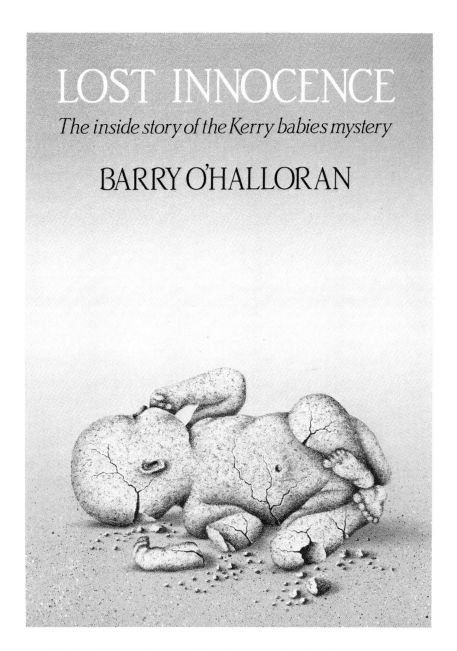

LOST INNOCENCE
The inside story of the Kerry babies mystery

BARRY O'HALLORAN

A broken doll provides a striking visual metaphor for a book cover dealing with the Kerry Babies case, published 1985.

Homage to Albrecht Dürer commissioned by the Dürer Haus in Nürnberg. A play on the use of perspective. Oil on canvas, 48 x 36.

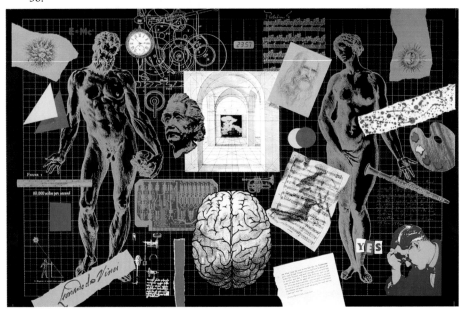

The Ambidextrous Paradigm. An innovative technique using printed circuit board technology to create art images, 1986. Silkscreen on copper etched board, 36 x 24.

change also made possible the future development of the museum, because now many art works could be brought to and displayed in one building. Also, this new mobility made possible the future establishment of an art market which would mirror the larger world of commerce."

By the twentieth century, revolutionary breakthroughs in technology began to prepare the way for yet another shift in the nature and form of art.

High-quality colour reproduction in books and magazines, amplified by the power of film, television and video to transmit and store pictures, have done away with the uniqueness of the art object by multiplying its accessibility.

As Walter Benjamin made clear in 'The Work of Art in the Age of Mechanical Reproduction', "images can now be ephemeral, ubiquitous, insubstantial, available, valueless, free."

What matters in art today is that for the first time people have the opportunity to see, enjoy and use images without ever needing to own the original works. Through reproduction art is becoming a normal part of everyone's environment.

Ballagh looks back with a certain amused detachment on his notorious tirade in *Hibernia,* castigating the role of galleries and dealers in making a prisoner of the artist.

"It was mad of me to worry so much about not being able to reach the public through the gallery system. It doesn't in fact matter that nobody goes to galleries except a small *élite.* If an artist sells his paintings through this system, that's fair enough. The important thing, which I didn't realise then, is that even if he sells a work, what the work says still belongs to him. It is completely separate from the art object used to carry it. It can still be disseminated to a universal audience through the printed image."

The implications of this have only slowly filtered through to artists: it is in the nature of social change only to become generally apparent in retrospect. One suspects that the move in the 1980s away from Modernism to more figurative forms — anticipated intuitively by Ballagh in the early 1970s — is in part a response to a growing awareness of the potential of the reproduced image.

"Of course there are elements in painting that cannot be transmitted by reproduction. But the reproduced image is different from the original rather than better or worse."

Ballagh's vision as an artist, formed by the cinematic and comic strip imagery of his childhood environment and later feeding on photographic sources, naturally lends itself to dissemination through reproduction. His adoption of the language of geometric perspective, which has been in common currency for over 500 years, heightens this affinity to popular communication: people readily accept it as a truthful way to depict reality.

In this he differs from more traditional Irish figurative painters like the late Maurice MacGonigal, who built up the paint with strong brushwork and allowed the colours to speak, or Patrick Collins, who hints at vague presences in a manner that loses much of its impact in reproduction.

"Most people seeing a reproduction of my work will get 100 per cent of what I'm trying to communicate."

This initially came about intuitively: he was only afterwards to rationalise the form his art has taken.

Reproduction brings a step further the process of democratisation begun by "Minister for Culture" David in opening up the Louvre to the public. It offers a way to reach the general public directly with art images. Through the medium of colour prints and colour TV every home can become a gallery.

As a commercial designer in the 1960s he had familiarised himself with the technical possibilities of print. Designing postage stamps throughout the 1970s later enabled him to develop considerable professional expertise in the various processes of colour reproduction. His first stamp, commissioned by the Stamp Design Advisory Council under Fr Donal O'Sullivan SJ, marked the World Meteorological Year in 1972. Since then he has become something of a stamp designer laureate, celebrating such national landmarks as the anniversaries of the ESB, the Boy Scouts and An Óige, the youth hostel movement.

"Stamps are difficult to do. The themes are often awkward to express. Typographical design can be difficult because philatelists love lots of information. Some kicked up a row over my scout stamps because, since the design was so obvious, I didn't use any explanatory words.

"My stamp celebrating the anniversary of the Bremen flight across the Atlantic was a particular challenge because I wanted to convey a feeling of a plane alone in a vast empty sky. But there's not that much space on a stamp!"

But all the time, working closely with the stamping branch of the

Revenue Commissioners, he has methodically built up his experience of what can be achieved in high-quality printing.

"I enjoy a relationship like that with somebody who is going to print something I'm doing. It gives me a sense of function."

Bureaucratic restriction on what can or cannot be attempted can sometimes be frustrating. He originally conceived the An Óige stamp in the shape of a triangle — the international symbol of the youth hostel movement. But the idea was turned down. There was a fear that post office workers might refuse to handle the new style stamp. Shortly before a George Bernard Shaw stamp had caused dissent because it was longer than normal.

The Poolbeg book cover commissions offered him much wider scope in the direct use of colour reproduction. Three of the covers were to be photographic treatments, the other three original paintings. For William Trevor's *The Distant Past,* a story about the way old wounds still bleed in Ireland, he used a variation of the image of shattered glass in *Miami Murders* and the Connolly portrait: a framed photograph of a British Army officer hangs askew in a drawing room, the glass pierced by a bullet, blood dripping down the wallpaper. Similarly the motif for Michael McLaverty's *Call My Brother Back* is derived from the chalk outlines of his 1972 Living Art gesture.

"You find that things cross-reference in your work and that an idea you've had in one medium may work in another."

Book covers have become a new medium for his political art: a way of reaching beyond the galleries in order to make more immediate contact with a general public.

Two particular examples of this were his covers for Donald Wood's *Black and White,* a polemic against the Irish Rugby Football Union's tour of South Africa — his image was a rugby ball as a bomb with a burning fuse — and for Tim Pat Coogan's *On the Blanket,* which provided a partisan account of the campaign for political status by Republican prisoners in the H-Block of the Maze Prison in the North.

His reaction to the emotive H-Block issue was conditioned, as with everything else, by a recognition of the dialectic of change.

"To me the loyalists in the North are not unlike the Afrikaaners — a people who have failed to adapt to the logic of history. If you try to deny all change, making the maintenance of an artificial status quo your *raison d'etre,* then you actually condemn yourself to no future.

You're taking an unhistorical position.

"The loyalists, like the European planters in Africa, sought to sustain their special position by force. They refused to share power or to integrate with the Catholic minority in the North. But they have only been able to do so, postponing the inevitable, with massive United Kingdom financial and military support.

"Compare what has happened in the South. The British planted Protestants here too, but in smaller numbers: they were always a minority. But they assimilated, became in many cases more Irish than the Irish themselves. The two communities are now able to live together without any of the suspicions and tensions that prevail in the North."

Gordon Lambert, a Protestant, was to tell him that people should weep for the murdered Protestants along the Border as well as for the dead hunger-striker Bobby Sands.

"Of course I wouldn't disagree. But in the long term, if we're ever to get to grips with the situation, we're going to have to look beyond the atrocities of the moment in order to take a broader historical view.

"Bobby Sands and the Provos exist because something is wrong. Fundamentally what is wrong is not Protestants being killed along the Border. Their suffering is a tragic symptom of the disease. The real problem is that the North as a unit doesn't work. The people who controlled it before the British imposed direct rule from Westminster are not entitled to run it because they are unwilling to compromise or to integrate. Integration is not a question of allowing the Catholic minority an odd job here or there or a few posts in a government. I firmly believe that the root cause is an unwillingness to live with their fellow human beings in a shared way. That's not compromise: it's the human condition."

Art like life is a process of change and assimilation: nothing stays the same. *Inside No 3* provided a fascinating glimpse of this coming together and interplay of influences from many different strands in Ballagh's own development as an artist and as a social being. It is the most complex and multi-layered work he has yet attempted.

With *No 3, Winter in Ronda* and *The Conversation,* the composition is architectural, presenting an elevation to scale of a building. *Inside No 3* defies this conventional visual logic, using several vanishing points to evoke the claustrophobic sense of being enveloped in a small room. The effect is to bend and distort perspective in a way similar to a fisheye photographic shot. Contouring the lines of the ceiling pulls the eye around in a circular motion in keeping with the theme he is presenting: the turning around of his own approach to painting.

Over the fireplace the framed reproduction of his stylised Pop version of the bare-breasted *Liberty at the Barricades* contrasts with the realistic nude study of Betty coming down the spiral staircase. The spiral has the effect of turning the eye from Betty to Liberty, creating an association between the two images. The fact that the Betty passage is based on Marcel Duchamp's *Abstracted Nude Descending Staircase* which in turn is derived from Muybridge's photographs of figures in motion is a subtle autobiographical reference to the derivation of his own images from photographic sources.

All that can be seen of Ballagh himself are his white shoes, resting on a couch, creating the illusion that he too is looking in with us on the painting — and on his own life — the focal point of his imagined eyes being a photographic image of himself on the TV screen. By his chair is a Fender guitar case, a nostalgic reminder of his pop music origins.

"What I enjoy about this kind of painting is that it works at different levels. Someone can appreciate it simply as a painting of a nude coming down a staircase without being aware of any of the

The doorway of the Ballagh house at No. 3 Temple Cottages.

other allusions. It has both artistic and personal layers."

It also, of course, communicates a social statement about the reality of being an artist in Ireland in the 1970s.

"Artists are mostly ordinary people in ordinary situations responding to ordinary things. They watch TV. They go shopping. They earn a living. Not at all as the popular mystique would have them."

His 1979 show at the David Hendriks Gallery, which included *Inside No 3, Winter at Ronda* and the portraits of Leonard, Greevy, Plunkett and Smith, was acclaimed as "one of the year's major artistic events" (to quote *In Dublin* magazine).

Brian Lynch in *Hibernia,* while admiring the virtuosity of the portraits ("a Dutch master of the still-life could hardly do better") thought the real successes were the personal pictures. *Winter in Ronda* was "quite clearly Ballagh's masterpiece, easily the best picture he's ever painted . . . The shadows on the cracked wall are as well handled as any impressionist and technically the whole thing shimmers beautifully . . . But what is really impressive is the complexity and the straightforwardness of the picture's emotions."

Desmond MacAvock in the *Irish Times* thought the work showed "noticeable development: the jokiness and cleverness have largely disappeared, or perhaps one should say are better integrated into the painting . . . the whole exhibition is a formidable, and fascinating display of energetic application and creativity."

Even Aidan Dunne in *In Dublin,* while disparagingly categorizing the work to date as "safe . . . acceptably modern . . . slickly illustrative . . . treading on a few toes . . . laboriously contrived with little sense of fluency or instinct", conceded that Ballagh was "moving in a useful direction, towards a preoccupation with painterly concerns. The introspection of the domestic pictures has undoubtedly had the paradoxical effect of broadening his scope."

Reaching this particular peak of achievement caused him to take a pause — as had often happened before — before again moving forward in a totally different direction.

8

He was approaching a mid-term stage in his career. During 1979 several events were to define his stature.

He was the only Irish artist, apart from New York-based Les Levine and English-based William Scott, represented in the extraordinary Museum of Drawers brought to Dublin by Herbert Distel that Spring. This was a representative collection of work commissioned from 500 of the top names in contemporary art, each of whom created a miniature small enough to fit into a 2 inch by 2 inch drawer in a cabinet.

Everyone from Picasso to Claes Oldenburg responded. There was an Andy Warhol silkscreen of Marilyn Monroe, a thumb print of Piero Manzoni, a Yves Klein blue stand, a Roy Lichtenstein jug, a David Hockney ink portrait, a Tom Wesselmann nude, a Jasper Johns Number 2.

As a joke Ballagh modelled a room in a modern art gallery in which three people are looking at paintings by Kenneth Noland and Ellsworth Kelly, two of a handful of artists who declined to participate because they feared the scale was too small to do justice to their hard-edge style.

This particularly delighted Distel. "Space is space, whatever its size," he told me. "The definition is the same, big or small."

Ballagh was also chosen with Louis le Brocquy to represent Ireland in Brussels in a major show organised to coincide with the first European Parliament election in May. He found himself in the same bracket as Francis Bacon, Paul Delvaux, Pierre Soulages, Graham Sutherland, Paul Wunderlich and Anthony Green.

An Arts Council touring exhibition of his political work between 1968-1978 was organised later in the year. "A goodish span to look back on, in order to make some kind of assessment," he remarked at the opening in the Orchard Gallery in Derry.

He was to do his rethinking not in Ireland but in the United States. He was one of fifteen visual art people from different parts of the world invited there by the State Department to tour galleries and art centres and to meet American artists in their studios and private workshops.

"The idea is to provide exposure to the contemporary art scene in the United States," Ambassador William Shannon explained.

The experience was if anything to confirm his disenchantment with Modernism.

"There was a terrifying rigidity everywhere we went. Nobody seemed to want to question anything. Modernism is the first art movement the Americans could claim to have invented — and that's why it got such a push. But what started off as a courageous radical idea became cemented into an establishment position totally unable to accept any other form of art.

"The Americans are the only people who could have conceived an art without tradition because they belong to a culture only two hundred years old. Newness *is* their tradition.

"I found it difficult to argue with anyone that both form *and* content were important in painting, that the two shouldn't be divorced. They didn't want to be told that the medium wasn't the message any more than the message wasn't the medium: that art was a duality of the two.

"Even Pop art, for all its irony, was stultified by the bland acceptance of everything irrespective of what it meant."

He listened politely to the Assistant Director of the lavishly endowed San Francisco Art Institute as she went on about all the wonderful facilities available for teaching art.

"Did you ever consider that the whole idea of an art college may be an anachronism," he remarked ironically.

There was a puzzled silence.

"Perhaps it might be a good idea to close them all down and to introduce an apprentice system similar to what they had during the Renaissance," he continued.

The subject was hastily changed. But the director made enquiries about him afterwards.

"Is he always like that?" she asked.

Seeing so much of the United States brought home to him for the first time how European he really was.

"A sense of the past and tradition are ingrained in our consciousness. Nations come and go. Everything changes. Nothing is really new."

One door had finally closed: the admiration of all things American. But another was to open. The journey across America provided a stimulus to use photography not just as a tool for his painting but as a form of expression in its own right.

He had brought his Rollei camera with the intention of simply recording what he saw, not being the kind of person to keep a diary. But he found he went for shots that didn't relate to any picture he was ever likely to paint. Invariably they were devoid of people.

"It takes me so long to take a picture, nobody would have waited. I'm a very slow and inexperienced photographer."

The very nature of his camera influenced the kind of photograph he was likely to take. Originally he had used the Rollei to collect images of figures for use in his series of people looking at paintings. But he also wanted to be able to keep a record of his work. The second-hand Rollei, which he bought for £25, was capable of taking larger size $2\frac{1}{4}$ inch square slides as distinct from the 35mm. variety.

"For an artist it's a very simple camera. It's totally manual. You use a light meter and then adjust the aperture and exposure. But it's literally only a box with a hole in front. You can't fit on any additional lenses or filters.

"I particularly like it because it's got twin lens reflex focussing. You simply look down and you can see on the $2\frac{1}{4}$ inch square ground glass a laterally reversed image of the picture you are taking This is useful if, like me, you wear glasses: they don't keep getting in your way. You can see much more than you would squinting through a 35mm. viewfinder. It's a perfect camera for composing a picture and for seeing exactly what you're going to close the shutter on."

He knew nothing about cameras to start with. By trial and error he discovered he could get the sharp definition he liked by always shooting at a small aperture. The huge depth of field, similar to that in his favourite old movies, did away with any fuzziness in the background or foreground: there was almost total focus throughout.

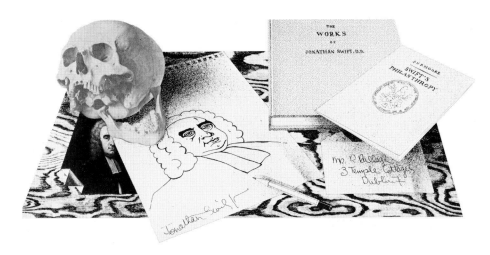

Sketch for a proposed portrait of Dean Swift for St Patrick's Hospital. Never realised.

"Photography has proved that the Renaissance painters weren't all that wrong in their way of presenting the illusion of the three-dimensional on a two-dimensional surface.

"The eye of twentieth-century man, nurtured on Western painting, was confirmed rather than changed by photography."

By the time he used it in the United States, the Rollei had become almost an extension of himself. He was taking photos on reflex. The American photos became a mirror of his preoccupation with architecure and with aspects of geometric perspective: dramatic angles of buildings against the sky and all the time a sense of looking through openings, doorways, windows, corridors, stairways.

All the film he shot was developed and printed up for him when he got back by David Davison, a lecturer in Photography at Kevin Street Technical College.

"I'm not interested in darkroom work. A photograph for me is all in the click of the shutter. If someone else can do a better job of printing my photographs, I don't see why I shouldn't use them. It's the quality of the image that matters, not the process by which it is produced.

"Over-dependence on technology can get in the way of using a camera as I feel it should be used. I don't like 'arty' photographs made by using lenses that distort or by shooting through glass with vaseline smeared on it. The eye is the thing. A camera should be like an eye."

Encouraged by Robin Berrington, the cultural officer at the American Embassy, he exhibited his American photographs at Kilkenny Arts Week and later at the David Hendriks gallery. It was the first time photographs had been shown there. Some people thought that they were out of place in a fine art setting.

"Painting and photography are just two different ways of creating images. There is no reason why one should be regarded as art and the other as something less."

Painters in the nineteenth century embraced the new medium of photography as a way of expanding their vision. To Delacroix it was "a remedy against mistakes". Yet there has always been a peculiar cultural prejudice against it. Many artists are hesitant to admit being influenced by it.

"Everyone takes snapshots. So people think it's just a matter of click click. There is a reluctance to accept that something mechanically produced can be a considered image."

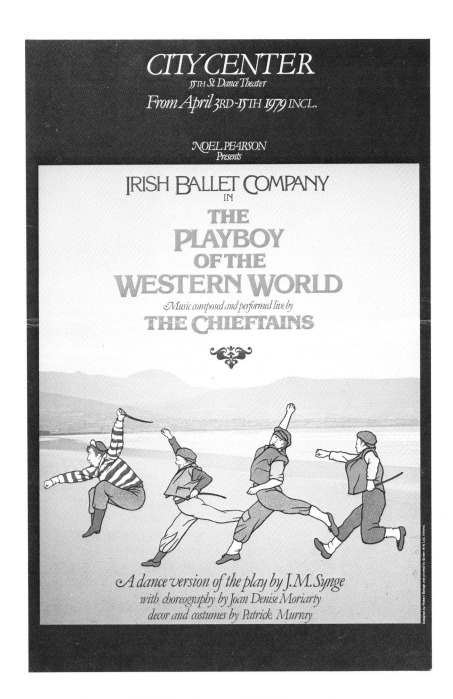

Poster for the Irish Ballet Company's 1979 Broadway debut.
Commissioned by one-time Chessmen manager Noel Pearson.

Yet a photographer is making choices all the time, selecting subjects, framing the composition, gauging the light, developing the negative, balancing the colour, cropping the print.

"If anything it's more difficult than painting because you have to deal concretely with reality. You can't paint away a lamp post that is not where you'd like it to be.

"My belief is that an artist stands or falls by what hangs on the wall. If the image is interesting and significant — or whatever one demands of a work of art — it doesn't matter whether he used X-ray film or charcoal on toilet paper to create it. It's the image that matters and what that image communicates to the observer."

Philip MacDermott, impressed by the personal feel of the photos, suggested a book of Dublin photos: not the usual Dublin of tourists but his own more intimate Dublin.

It was a chance to add another dimension to the personal exploration he had begun in his painting. As with the American photos, he avoided the inclusion of people. But this time it became a conscious decision. People automatically became the focus of attention in a photograph. He wanted instead to catch a sense of place: the aura of the streets around Broadstone where he lived, the Herbert Park and Sandymount Strand he remembered from childhood, the Vico Road and White Rock he sketched as a student with Michael O'Sullivan.

9

Photography for a while monopolised his creative energies. He was to complete only four paintings in 1980 and 1981, all of them commissioned portraits. There were paintings in his mind he was eager to start. But bills had to be met. He had to make a living.

"It's a frustrating experience. It takes so long between thinking of an image and being able to get it down on canvas. If ideas are let fester too long, they may lose their freshness."

He doesn't regret the time he has spent on portraits. They are to him an equally valid part of his development as a painter.

"I don't regard commissions as being inferior or superior to my other work. But there is a danger, as happened with William Orpen, of getting so involved with commissions that you're left without time or energy for anything else. Yet there are areas you can't reach in

The Decade of Endeavour. Portrait of Charles Haughey, receiving the acclaim of the Fianna Fail Ard Fheis, 1980, after his political comeback. Oil on canvas, 60 x 48.

commissioned work, that you can only tease out by following your own course."

But some commissions are too intriguing to decline.

Charles Haughey, after his dramatic triumph in the Fianna Fail leadership struggle late in 1979, appointed the poet Anthony Cronin as a cultural adviser to the Government. It was an initiative in keeping with his record as Minister for Finance in the 1960s when he had introduced a tax free scheme for writers and artists. Now as Taoiseach he intended to introduce with the help of Cronin and the Arts Council a scheme called Aosdána whereby artists in need could receive a £5,000 tax-free salary from the State in addition to their normal earnings from their art.

It seemed appropriate as a patron of the arts — completely out of the traditional run of Irish politicians — to commission a portrait of himself from a young Irish artist. Cronin suggested Ballagh. They had established a rapport on a lecture tour in the United States. They shared similar ideas on the function of the artist as a recorder of the changing face of society.

Back in the 1950s Cronin had written in *Envoy:* "the natural focal point for every poet is his own position in the world, and if he expresses his feelings about that accurately he is doing as good a political job as anyone else."

Ballagh carries the quote around in his wallet. "It confirms for me what I am doing in my painting."

The brief specified the Fianna Fáil Ard Fheis of 1980: the acclamation of Haughey's return to power after years in the political wilderness following the Arms Trial. This didn't leave great scope for originality. The paraphernalia of leadership would have to be shown: microphones, cheering and waving, the huge magnified photograph of the party leader dwarfing the speakers. The colours too were fixed: blue, green and orange.

"Perhaps they make an impact on TV. But they are not effective in an art work."

He visited Haughey at his mansion at Kinsealy and at the Taoiseach's office for photo sessions. They had met casually a few times before now but he got to know the man behind the public image.

"I began to appreciate how he could elicit so much loyalty. He had the common touch. He didn't have to put it on. He really seemed to enjoy the whole necessary political business of shaking hands and kissing babies."

To emphasise the presidential style of leadership Ballagh eliminated all the ministers who would normally share the platform with Haughey, leaving him to stand alone beneath an enormous blow-up photographic image of himself. Hands wave tricolours and conference papers in the foreground: the simulated hysteria of Party acclaim.

Ballagh at the same time worked on a small portrait of the architect Michael Scott who, with Robin Walker, had been one of his first patrons, commissioning the UCD cafeteria screens in 1970. He used a variation of the Greevy approach, pinning on to a drawing board documentation from Scott's varied career as an internationally-acclaimed architect. There were photographs of some of the buildings he had designed — including Dublin's bus terminal — a catalogue from ROSC, which he had started in 1967, a programme for Dublin Theatre Festival, of which he was Chairman, and, of course, the tools of his profession: T-square, pencil, rubber and set-square. The likeness of Scott was presented in the form of a colour snapshot.

Each Ballagh portrait has to be seen in relation to all the others. They are not one-off works but part of a series of paintings in which the common theme is portraiture. Just as he paints series of people looking at paintings, or of iced caramels and liquorice allsorts, or of Third Policeman images, so has he painted a series of portrait images. The fact that they are commissioned and his other art isn't, is relevant only in so far as it is in the nature of a portrait to be commissioned.

It is not possible to comprehend fully Ballagh's development as an artist without detailed consideration of all his commissioned work: through commissions of all kinds he has time and again received the stimulus and the experience to develop the theme and the language that enrich the pictures he paints for himself. The challenge of a deadline or of a specific brief draws out his innovative powers. But this can happen only if a balance can be maintained between the two

A general view of Ballagh's retrospective in the Municipal Gallery of Lund, Sweden, in early 1983.

areas of work. By 1981 this balance had become dangerously lopsided. Commissions were taking up virtually all his time.

"I felt a need to back away from the portraits and to develop more personal themes I had in mind. But I couldn't afford the inevitable loss of income this would entail."

The problem was resolved by the £3,000 Martin Toonder Award which he received from the Arts Council that August. It bought him the time to embark on the two paintings he had long before completed in his imagination.

Since breaking with Modernism his painting was autobiographical on two different levels. *No 3, Winter in Ronda* and *Inside No 3* were concerned with the intimate side of his life as a family man and a painter. *My Studio 1969* and *The Conversation* were a more general exploration of his role as an artist in society. With *Upstairs No 3* he would take the domestic series a stage further, while he hoped to expand the dialogue on the nature of art — particularly the whole question of Irishness in art — in a painting tentatively entitled *The Pause That Refreshes* and eventually completed in 1983 as *Highfield*.

He was one of the first established artists to break with Modernism and to develop a more personal kind of art, re-affirming the relevance of the figurative image. This in the 1980s is now becoming the new international aesthetic. Painting is coming back into its own. There is a gradual move "to reconnect", as Ballagh has done, with the enduring traditions of western art.

"It is surely unthinkable that the representation of human experience, in other words people and their emotions, landscapes and still lives, could forever be excluded from painting," proclaimed the manifesto for the 1981 *A New Spirit in Painting* exhibition at the Royal Academy in London. "They must in the long run again return to the centre of the argument of painting."

This is the paradox of art in the 1980s: new is old and old is new. There is no longer One True Faith. Dogmatism has given way to diversity. Messages of taste are no longer handed down from New York or Paris or wherever: the challenge to artists everywhere is to create their own.

Ballagh is one of the few Irish artists to draw with any consistency on personal experience to make universal statements, an achievement underlined by international reaction to ROSC 80.

Die Welt critic Hanns Theodor Flemming noted with

disappointment "how strongly regional art production in Ireland has been shaped by international trends and how people everywhere try at all costs to make or hold the connection with the supposedly *avant-garde* tendencies . . .

"If we look for specifically Irish components among the Irish artists we find everywhere the echoes of Celtic spiral ornamentation or of the shapes of the early Christian stone crosses in many transfigurations, but hardly any independent works of contemporary character.

"One exception is Robert Ballagh, who was born in Dublin in 1943 and who allows one to perceive in his paintings, which are stylistically situated between old masters and Pop art, a specifically Irish irony and a choice of themes which is full of critically conscious allusions.

"In one of his works he himself poses among his young family studying Velazquez, while in the pile of books beside him is James Joyce's *Ulysses.* Another picture called *The Conversation* shows Ballagh in a modernised Dutch interior talking to Vermeer's self-portrait from behind which appears the famous artist's studio scene from 1666. In front of the papered and empty wall is a stretched canvas with the initials RB77 which has been taken off the wall and turned around leaving a clear patch on the wallpaper. The canvas has an illusory tangible quality about it.

"It is rare to find artists today capable of such well-executed self-irony and cultural criticism."

Jack Lynch, the former Taoiseach, painted for a Magill cover, 1980.

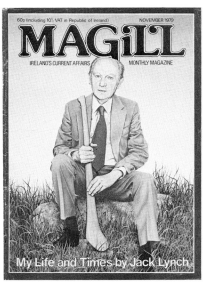

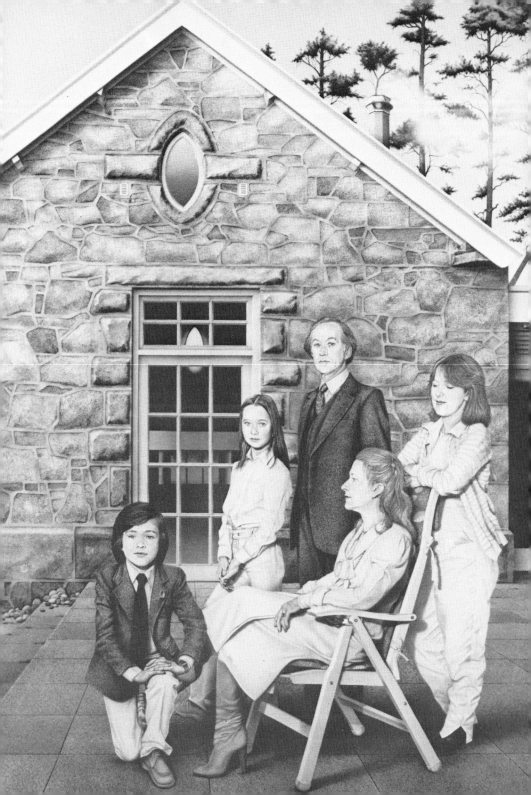

5

"Subversion is more effective if it is expressed in an accessible language"

1

A party at Gordon Lambert's home in Rathfarnham. The purpose is to make a presentation to Basil Goulding who is ill. Some months later he would die of cancer.

The guests, all close friends from the Contemporary Irish Art Society, which Basil had founded in the 1960s, mingle through the rooms and in the garden, admiring a new totem-like Eilis O'Connell sculpture.

Margaret Downes singles out Robert Ballagh in a room dominated by a dazzling Vasarely. She and Desmond want changes in the figurative elements of the portrait, which he had shown them for the first time a few days before.

"It would ruin the picture to make any radical changes," Ballagh tells her.

After this deadlock ensues. The portrait remains in the David Hendriks Gallery during the summer.

Ballagh is plainly annoyed. But he reacts eventually in his usual pragmatic way.

"I'm not one to go away and behave irrationally."

After experimenting with some additional glazing, he again delivers the portrait. This time the Downses are happy to accept it.

"It's not the function of an artist to behave in a precious way. He's a tradesman doing a job like anyone else. He deals with each situation as he finds it. He has no claim to any privileged status."

2

Ballagh still had another portrait to complete: the Mallin family in

The completed Downes portrait, with detail of the figures. Oil on canvas, 48 x 60.

179

The Mallin Family. The setting is the space in their sitting room where the portrait now hangs. Oil on canvas, 48 x 60.

their sitting room. The setting is the actual space where the finished portrait will eventually hang: yet another chance to play with repeating images. The portrait within the portrait on the wall behind the figures is a preparatory drawing for the portrait itself. Within that, in place of the drawing, is a piece of unprimed canvas.

"It's a reference to the time-scale involved in a work like this and to the whole process of creating images."

The device is not completely arbitrary. The sense of openings within openings connects with Mallin's business as an importer of doors and window fittings and with Ballagh's own experience as a draughtsman with Milners designing metal windows.

The Mallin and the Downes portraits — in effect ten separate portraits in terms of actual figures — absorbed all his painting time for nearly a year.

Portrait of Gay Byrne. The Kodak transparency format alludes to Byrne's interest in photography. Oil on canvas, 16 x 16.

"When I accepted these commissions I didn't realise how difficult they would prove to be. All my previous portraits had been of people with public personas to which I could readily respond. With the family portrait I had entered the private domain, where my task was obviously more difficult."

They were portraits in the more traditional sense of the genre. They held the mirror up to the Irish bourgeoisie.

"Hopefully they will tell something about the society of the time."

He resolved to suspend doing commissioned work for a while and return to doing autobiographical pictures.

But first Gordon Lambert wanted a small surprise portrait of Gay Byrne to celebrate his twenty years in Irish television. It would be presented at the annual Jacob Awards.

"I'd met Gay Byrne on the *Late Late* show at the time my Dublin photographs were published and I discovered he had a passionate interst in photography. I took my idea from that."

The portrait is in the form of a Kodachrome slide. Byrne's head is highlighted against a sky that fades from night to day, a neat visual reference to his p.m. television and a.m. radio slots. Ballagh's name is printed in the peeled back corner in the familiar yellow and red Kodak lettering.

With this out of the way he was finally free to see through an idea that had been nagging him since *No 3* in 1977.

But it didn't happen the way he planned.

He'd always intended to complete the *No 3* series with *Upstairs No 3.* Yet now a completely different painting suggested itself.

It started out as a title with a pun.

"We'd had the house redecorated while we were on holidays in Spain the previous summer.

"This prompted me to relate the idea of modernising a home to the whole concept of post-Modernism."

Inside No 3, After Modernisation allows a plethora of styles to co-exist in a way that makes visual sense. Ballagh, painted in the realist manner he now favours, sits at a table in his changed home. On the wall a Jackson Pollock pastiche provides a splurge of abstract expressionism. Leopard skin covers recall the punk imagery of his kitsch show in the early 1970s. The number 3 in the top left corner is pure Art Deco. The furniture is delineated with the formalist black line he once shared with Patrick Caulfield. The whole composition has a Cubist tilt.

"The plurality of styles reflects the reality artists are now experiencing. They're no longer under pressure to fit in with any particular 'ism'. They can draw on all sorts of different things to make images they consider relevant."

The bold shapes and colours enabled him to go back to using the acrylics he abandoned during the "people looking at pictures" series.

"Having done two very complicated portraits, I needed a holiday from detail. I wanted to be able to paint something quickly."

But once under way, *After Modernisation* became something more than he had intended. There are no easy pictures any more.

He has depicted himself with an elbow on a book entitled *After Modernism*, obviously pondering the future of art. A copy of *Das Kapital* points to a possible way forward: the need to reassert the social responsibilty of the artist. Ballagh is again rejecting the role of the artist as a romantic outsider, alienated from the rest of society, baring his soul for future generations.

"All that belongs to the 19th century. Modernism clung to it long after it had any relevance. American artists liked to see themselves as heroes in a cultural western, living like Jackson Pollock on the edge, pushing the frontiers of art.

"The truth is that the effective frontiers for art today are all in our heads. The artist will better articulate either the conscious or the unconscious concerns of the people if he is one of the people."

Modernism tried to shock people out of their minds by doing outrageous things: its challenge was essentially formal. "What's needed now is to make what we're actually saying shocking so that people can understand and see what they're being shocked with.

"I'm not saying that artists shouldn't still, as Marcuse said, name the unnameable. But subversion is more effective if it is expressed in an accessible language."

Like the novels of Gabriel Garcia Marquez, which are shocking in their content rather than their form. In *Autumn of the Patriarch,* for instance, a general is brought in stuffed and then eaten.

"Marquez's surreal vision of Latin American dictatorships is more real than a lot of realistic accounts. He is challenging us in what he says rather than how he says it."

This is the way Ballagh would like his images to function, the direction all his later work has taken.

"The painting may be simple on the surface but it should have a lot going on in it."

The social responsibility of the artist goes beyond what he puts on canvas. If the artist in Ireland today still feels like an outsider it is partly because he has allowed himself to be shut out.

"All the country's legislation, with the exception of Section 2 of the 1969 Finance Act, has been drawn up without any consideration of the working conditions or the status of the artist."

Ballagh discovered this the hard way when he tried to go on the dole only to discover that there were no Social Welfare provisions for the artist. He was technically a non-person when it came to applying for benefits.

"In effect you are unable to claim what other members of the community are entitled to by right. You're thrown back on the very lowest end of the social welfare system or else forced to rely on help from friends."

Late in 1981 a group of artists sought to end this anomaly by forming the Association of Artists in Ireland. Initially they were encouraged and assisted by David Kavanagh of the Arts Council. The first committee of Michael O'Sullivan, Eithne Jordan, Vivienne Roche, Cathy Carman, Patrick Hall, Jim Allen, Leo Higgins and Ken Dolan, with Ballagh as chairman, quickly affiliated with the Cultural Division of the Irish Transport and General Workers' Union, following discussions with Dermot Doolin. Offices were provided in Liberty Hall — Betty was appointed administrator — and two members were appointed to the committee of the Cultural Division to join representatives from Actors Equity, The Society of Irish Playwrights, The Association of Irish Composers and other cultural workers.

"By avoiding all the usual aesthetic arguments and by concerning ourselves instead with strictly professional matters, we've managed to appeal to the whole spectrum of artists whether academicians or *avant garde.*"

By early 1983 the Association had a membership of over 160. Meetings were held with various government departments regarding Income Tax, VAT, Social Welfare benefits and Customs and Excise regulations.

"All the people we talked with were extremely sympathetic. But they have to deal with the legislation as it exists."

The ITGWU is the first trade union to have an arts policy, adopted unanimously by its annual conference. Through its Cultural Division it has been involved in preparing comprehensive cultural documents based on EEC and UNESCO experience which will be presented to the Government and other interested parties recommending detailed legislative changes needed to bring the position of the artist in Ireland into line with that of artists in other European countries.

Meanwhile piecemeal improvements have been achieved.

The Arts Council has given support to the campaign for re-sale rights by agreeing to pay artists five per cent on any paintings subsequently resold from their collection.

With the help of John Gore-Grimes standard contracts have been drawn up to facilitate artists in their dealings with galleries and the public.

"People don't seem to appreciate that buying art is no different to buying anything else. When you buy a suit you don't expect to get it for months on approval and then be allowed to give it back."

The Association has taken successful action on behalf of artists in a number of cases of non-payment for paintings.

ASSOCIATION OF ARTISTS IN IRELAND

Ballagh and playwright Brian Friel were appointed to the Arts Council in summer 1982 following representations to the then Taoiseach Charles Haughey and served until early 1984.

"We argued that cultural workers should have representatives on any decision-making body that affects their profession." Involvement in trade union matters has inevitably eaten into the time Ballagh has for his art, much more so than committee work for the Exhibition of Living Art or the monthly meetings of the Municipal Gallery advisory committee.

"It's frustrating in a way but I saw it as a short-term commitment.

"To use the biblical phrase, the cup is passed your way once in your life and if you have a sense of responsibility you must accept it."

4

The impulse to censor is inherent in the treatment of the nude in Western art: the legacy of the fig-leaf.

There has always been a half-guilty reticence — not found in Indian or Japanese graphic art — in dealing with erotic subject-matter in a non-pornographic way.

Ballagh remembers how priests at Blackrock College would black out nude details on the colour slides of Renaissance masterpieces shown in art appreciation lectures.

The nude is tolerated in a strictly aesthetic context: to go beyond that is considered demeaning.

The fact that greater licence is allowed in the depiction of the female as distinct from the male nude merely mirrors the subordinate role of women in society.

Upstairs No 3 is a calculated challenge to that ambivalence.

Ballagh had reluctantly taken up the issue during the public outcry over his kite of a flasher. "But the ground was not of my choosing. The whole thing became trivialised."

Inside No 3 employed the image of a female nude descending a staircase, a recurring theme in Western painting (Ballagh's particular reference was to Marcel Duchamp). With *Upstairs No 3* he undermines the assumptions of the genre by reversing the sex roles: instead of a nude descending, he shows himself nude coming up into the bedroom.

Betty is lying naked on a bed with an illustrated book of Japanese erotic art open on her lap. The composition is structured, by leaving her head out of the picture, to create the illusion that she is the observer, just as Ballagh was in *Inside*.

"The concept of the female nude frontally exposed to the observer is rooted in male attitudes. Often she was the mistress of the king or the patron, as John Berger has argued, and was painted to look out at her owner." By switching to a woman's viewpoint Ballagh is attempting to overturn that tradition.

"Not that a man can ever really paint what a woman sees or thinks. When James Joyce wrote Molly Bloom's soliloquy he came close to achieving this aim."

The Japanese or "pillow picture" that Betty is admiring is a reminder that beyond the Western tradition of art there are other, perhaps more honest, ways of dealing with erotic subject matter.

Ballagh painted it to scale from a reproduction of a colour print by Shuncho, who was responsible for some of the most beautiful erotic pictures of the late 18th century.

"There is a complete absence of the proprietary response one associates with the Western treatment of the female nude.

"The two people — there are always two in *shunga* art — are involved with themselves and unconcerned with the observer. They are looking at each other rather than at us."

Nudity is too commonplace in Japan — the country of communal bathing — to be considered erotic. It rarely features in their art. The figures in shunga pictures are invariably draped. Only the genitalia are exposed, their proportions greatly exagggerated in order to concentrate attention on the sexual activity, the real purpose of the picture.

Such pictures were frequently given to newly-weds: they were expressly intended for the pleasure of the viewer. As Richard Illing points out in *Japanese Erotic Art,* "The Japanese never considered that sexual enjoyment was something to which shame should attach."

By contrasting Eastern and Western sexual imagery in this way Ballagh is making a further comment on art: that it cannot avoid being a social product, a mirror of its time and place.

The explicit sexual details caused him some worry. But it would have been a contradition of terms to have pulled back coyly from the logical implications of the theme.

The circular format of the composition sustains the dialogue with *Inside No 3* which, although square, used several vanishing points to convey a tremendous spiral feeling.

Technically *Upstairs* is square too: the circle is projected on a black background. "Circular stretchers are very tricky. I discovered that the hard way with the Ingres *Turkish Bath.* They're expensive too. You also need hand-carved frames. The alternative is to leave it unframed and I've learned to my cost that paintings have to be framed if they're to have any life at all. Otherwise they get hacked around the edges."

A ¼-inch thick gold-leaf border alienates what is going on inside the circle from the black background: the effect is like looking into the lens of a camera. Yet again the solution to a purely practical problem has enhanced his visual language.

Facing Betty on the wall is a reproduction of *Rue de Paris: Temps de pluie* by the Impressionist Gustave Caillebotte, a painting that could never have been visualised without the invention of photography. The wide angle view of the street and the cropping of the figures and the buildings suggests the effect of the lens of a camera.

"The reproduction actually hangs in the same position as I have shown it. I didn't just put it there for the painting."

Its function is to assert an essentially urban way of looking at the world that has an affinity with his own. It draws attention to the subtle way in which our vision has come to be conditioned by the camera.

"Caillebotte is one of my favourite 19th-century realist painters."

Through the bedroom window we catch a glimpse of the King's Inns building.

"Not quite the actual view. You'd have to go to the top of the street to see it like that. But I wanted to do justice to Gandon's architecture."

A US combat helicopter — a Huey Cobra from *Apocalypse Now* — hovers menacingly above, a fairly obvious anti-militarist statement.

"Helicopter gunships have replaced the cavalry in the American psyche. To me they represent increasingly aggressive international attitudes and governmental hostility to the peace movement.

"But the idea of depicting helicopters over the King's Inns is not pure fantasy. The Inns lies directly on the line between the Special Criminal Courts and Mountjoy prison. During political trials helicopters regularly sweep the area."

A stylised portrait of James Connolly — the image used on the cover of *International Socialism* – reiterates the political intention of *Upstairs No 3*. It is appropriately placed on the wall directly behind Ballagh as he stands facing us at the top of the spiral. The circular shape, while confirming the overall composition, can also be seen as a visual metaphor for what seems to be Ballagh's underlying

Portrait of Michael Scott. Documentation of the architect's
career pinned to a drawing board. Oil on canvas, 36 x 36.

theme: the sense of turning back in order to reassert the beliefs that
shape and motivate him as an artist in society.

He has always shown a wariness about being absorbed by the
establishment, remembering Che Guevara's jibe about performing
monkeys.

"What I'm trying to say is that whatever way I fit into the social
context, my allegiance to Connolly and to Irish socialism is not
going to waver.

"The game may get more complex, but my views remain the
same."

5

"Jag tillhör inte dem som skar av sitt óra for Konstens skull . . . "
("I'm not the kind to cut off my ear for art . . . ").

Ballagh's rejection of the role of the artist as hero was to become the manifesto for a major retrospective of his work in Sweden in February 1983. He had participated in a group show "From Yeats to Ballagh" at Lund Municipal Gallery in 1982. Now the curator Marianne Manne-Brähammer invited him back. For months he had been supervising the preparation and shipment of the 80 works selected by her: an eerie experience.

"I didn't know what I was letting myself in for. It's a bit like drowning; you see all your life flashing before you."

It was coming at an apt time. He had wrapped up the *No 3* series with *Upstairs No 3*. He would be forty later in the year. He was mid-career.

"My old paintings now seem as if they have been painted by someone else. Seeing them again makes me realise that I've reached some sort of turning-point."

As he tidied up the studio before flying out with Betty for the opening, it was as if he was doing it for the last time. His landlord had demanded a steep increase in rent. Disputing it in court was only putting off the inevitable. Soon it would no longer make economic sense to continue working in Parliament Street.

Inside No 3, After Modernisation leant against the wall, ready for his exhibition in the David Hendriks Gallery in March. *Upstairs No 3* still needed a final varnish. He would touch it up when he got back.

A canvas stood beneath the skylight with the outline of the next painting, *The Pause That Refreshes* (a phrase culled from an old American coke advertisement subliminally associating the product with the fresh air of the great outdoors). It showed him beside an easel at the door of their cottage at Ballybraher, near Ballycotton, Cork. Photographs of the view were pinned to the side for reference.

"It will be an attempt to explore the whole idea of Irishness in art. But I'm not yet sure how I'll do it. All I know is that the lovely view I'm looking out on will not be what I'm putting on canvas. The point is that although I'm attracted to the Irish landscape it's not and never was part of my cultural tradition. I can't draw on it in my art and still be honest with myself."

A torn-up Picasso poster — *A Portrait of Jacqueline,* which Godard used in his movie *Pierrot le fou* – was discarded on the floor.

"As if to say that is not the way for me either."

The composition of the picture was a reversal of *Winter in Ronda:* a looking out instead of in.

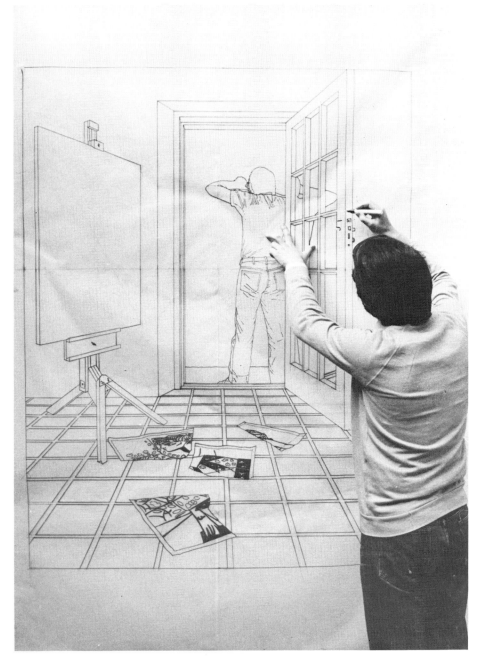

Highfield. Ballagh at work in his studio, summer 1983. The
painting was completed in 1984.

"It provides an opportunity to paint the kind of painting I've been dying to do for years. What the French call *contre jour*, painting into the light. Casper Friedrich did it a lot. You can get a lovely effect with the figure; light flaring at the edges."

He tapped the empty area of the painting within the painting. "But I can't make up my mind what to put here.

"Perhaps I'll just leave it blank."

The solution could be the key to the picture.

And perhaps also to the direction his art is about to take.

But there were to be many interruptions before he completed it nearly a year later.

Soon after his return from Sweden he headed an AAI delegation (which included Betty and Samuel Walsh) to the annual congress in Helsinki of the UNESCO-affiliated International Association of Artists, where he was unexpectedly voted on to the 16-member executive committee for a three-year term of office.

"It was wholly against the political odds. After all, we were only newcomers among the 81 member countries in contention. I think we were welcomed by the various blocs as an independent voice."

Overnight he became a spokesman for artists not only in Ireland but throughout the world. "Who would have thought I'd finish up addressing a UNESCO meeting in Paris on the role of culture in third world development!" Certainly not the management of Milners whom he had confronted in the Labour Court as a youthful trade unionist. There were meetings too in East Berlin and the Soviet Union. The Castro regime invited him to Cuba to address an international seminar on painting. It was like going home: Cuban graphic art and the ideas of Che Guevara had conditioned his thinking as a painter in the formative years in the late 1960s. In early November 1985 he attended the annual meeting of the IAA in Tokyo: a chance to see at first hand the Japanese art that was a source for *Upstairs No 3*.

The AAI would exploit these visits to open up cultural exchanges with other countries. Cuban graphics were to tour Ireland in 1986 with a reciprocal exhibition of Irish graphics going to Cuba.

"All this international contact has given us greater clout at home. It's now becoming normal to include artists in the decision-making process in matters concerning the arts."

Particularly since the publication early in 1985 of the AAI's "Crisis in the Arts" report which, drawing on information provided by artists groups abroad, forcefully argued the case for a specific Government policy on the arts.

"The thing that strikes you in countries like Cuba is that the arts are expected to play a significant part in the social life of the community and that consequently there are plans and very definite policies for the arts."

By contrast the Coalition Government's three-year National Plan made no reference whatsoever to the arts.

Just as the Lemass/Whitaker prosperity boom of the 1960s generated a buoyant market for art among the newly affluent middle classes and image-conscious corporations, the recession of the 1980s all but wiped it out. By August 1985 unemployment had soared to 235,000 or a massive 17.7 per cent of the labour force. An income freeze combined with punitive tax rates to put even the average industrial worker into the super-tax bracket.

"The impact of the recession has severely curtailed the private patronage of the arts to the extent that now most visual artists can expect little financial return through sales and commissions," warned the "Crisis in the Arts" report.

With *Inside No 3, After Modernisation* and *Upstairs No 3* — effectively a year's work — lying unsold in the Hendriks gallery, Ballagh had no option but to fall back again on commissions to suport his family.

Everyone kept advising him to paint small. With his facility with paint, there was no doubt he could easily oblige and there would be ready buyers. But instead he stayed with the large-scale *The Pause That Refreshes,* now retitled simply *Highfield.*

He has decided to leave the painting within the painting blank after all. "Because it works as a questioning picture. The questions it raises about the role of the artist and about cultural identity in Ireland are questions, not answers." He filled it with the kind of light that bathed *Winter in Ronda.* It shared the Spanish painting's same seductive blue clarity.

David Hendriks did not live to see it completed, dying of cancer in October 1983. There would be no more lively chats at his famous desk which backed the high Georgian windows overlooking Stephens Green. But the gallery survived with the support of businessman and collector Vincent Ferguson. *Highfield* featured at the re-opening group show the following spring.

Even if his major original works failed to sell in 1985, the images reached an international audience. *Upstairs No 3* and *After Modernisation* toured the United States in an exhibition of Irish art chosen by New York critic Lucy Lippard. He had work in the Varna Print Biennale in Bulgaria, exhibitions of Irish prints in China and Milwaukee, and in an Artists Association show in Tokyo. A small fish-eye self-portrait, recalling a much earlier effort as a 16-year-old schoolboy, was chosen for the Sofia Triennale of Realist Art.

He lived a stone's throw from the Four Courts. A brief from the Association of Criminal Lawyers to portray retiring District Justice Robert Ó hUadhaigh gave him a chance to correct the romantic notion of the courts as places rich in the ceremony of time-honoured traditions. For the majority of cases the reality is much more banal.

He spent several days in District Court No 6 observing Ó hUadhaigh, a man noted for the consistency and firmness of his verdicts. "He's one of the real characters, respected even by the criminals for his abrasiveness and humour."

The simple portrait shows him without a gown or wig, looking to one side as if asking his clerk what he should do next. The mood is matter-of-fact and routine. "It's intended as the image of a judge in Ireland at this stage of the 20th century." It fitted in neatly with Ballagh's notion of portraiture as a social record of its time.

The marriage of modernism with the Renaissance sense of perspective characterised by *The Conversation* had drawn comment in Germany during Rosc. Dr. Karl Heinz Schreyl, head of the Dürer Haus in Nurmberg, visiting Dublin for the opening of a Dürer exhibition at the Chester Beatty library, made a point of viewing *The Conversation* which had been praised for its Vermeer references by the *Die Welt* critic. He promptly commissioned a similar homage to Dürer for a room in the museum devoted to artists influenced by him.

Rather than turn for inspiration to the familiar Dürer self-portrait or his study of Adam and Eve, Ballagh focussed on a celebrated series of illustrations on perspective. Dürer had been one of the first artists in the 16th century to draw up diagrams and systems to depict perspective. In one of the illustrations he portrayed an artist using a grid to draw a reclining nude in foreshortened perspective. Making a play on *The Conversation,* Ballagh repeats this image, but substituting himself for the artist: a 20th-century artist in jeans and white sneakers in a Renaissance art setting. The unveiling of the work in Nürnberg was widely reported with reproductions

Portrait of District Justice O hUadhaigh. Oil on canvas, 42 x 30.

published in newspapers throughout Germany with the caption "Irish irony".

The irony didn't end at that. The image became unexpectedly self-fulfilling. On returning to Dublin Ballagh found that the cottage next door to No 3 had become vacant. He managed to put together enough money to acquire it for conversion into a studio. Like Dürer and other Renaissance painters he now lived over the shop.

The Dublin book of photographs had meanwhile attracted the attention of the Limited Editions Club in New York which specialised in commissioning leading international artists to illustrate classic literary works. Among the writers and artists on their lists were Gunter Grass, Jose Luis Borges, Seamus Heaney, Sol Lewitt and David Hockney. He was invited to provide a series of photographs for their new edition of Joyce's *Dubliners* with an introduction by Thomas Flanagan. As with his prints of Trinity College, the Rotunda Hospital and the facade of an old church in Stephen's Green which had been converted into the new Smurfit Paribas bank, this offered another welcome opportunity to relate to his city through the detail of its buildings.

This affinity for Dublin was also to find expression in his first attempt at stage design. Actor Barry McGovern and the Beckett scholar Gerry Dukes had devised a one-man show for the 1985 Dublin Theatre Festival based on the trilogy of novels, *Molloy, Malone Dies* and *The Unnameable,* with former Arts Council director Colm Ó Briain directing. With his customary flair Michael Colgan, the ebullient force behind the Gate Theatre's resurgence in the mid-1980s, recalling how Diaghilev had encouarged avant-garde painters like Picasso to collaborate with the Ballets Russe, invited Ballagh to create a set.

"Colm was keen to sustain a certain narrative logic so that the piece would have a oneness about it. The idea was to follow the inherent structure of the trilogy rather than take excerpts.

"The more I absorbed myself in Beckett the more I realised that less is more. Ideally all that was needed was just an actor saying those wonderful words and anything else would be an unnecessary extra. But of course you have to have something else."

So he came up with something that is almost not there: a cube space delineated by a rim of neon light.

"Drawing with light is total abstraction. Establishing a space for Barry in this way rather than obeying naturalistic conventions

Ballagh's neon light set heightens the impact of Barry McGovern's performance in the Beckett show *I'll Go On* at the Gate. Ballagh is shown with a preliminary working model for the set.

would be much more in keeping with Beckett's work. The least amount of clutter seemed essential. You don't want to presume to add anything to Beckett."

The show became one of the critical and box-office hits of the festival. "Likely to travel beyond Ireland's borders," predicted *Time* magazine. Which it did. It was invited to Paris to celebrate Beckett's 80th birthday the following April and later that year to the Edinburgh Festival.

But Ballagh, unlike Hockney, does not regard stage design as a significant outlet for his art. "My imagination goes more in the direction of pop videos rather than dressing up a stage for a play and chasing around trying to get tea cosies with the right period feel."

7

He didn't set out to crucify Noel Browne. His portrait of the 70-year-old Socialist standing in front of his cottage in Connemara simply happened that way. The cruciform shape was the most practical way to paint it.

"When I started working the picture out first, it was going to be a full rectangle." But this would have meant painting acres of stones. So he took away the sides, giving greater emphasis to the tall figure.

Then he looked at the top corners, which were just empty sky. That had to come out too. "It was only then I realised that I'd finished up with a very emotive shape that had obvious spiritual connotations.'

He left it on the drawing board for a couple of months before deciding to go ahead.

"By using what is seen by many people as a very strong religious image in a totally secular way I could turn a lot of things on their head."

The effect is savagely ironic.

Browne's gaze is as uncompromising as the bleak landscape around him. Here is a man who has stood his ground.

As Minister for Health in the first Inter-Party Government he resigned rather than go along with his colleagues in abandoning the Mother and Child Health Scheme because it had been denounced by the Hierarchy as "opposed to Catholic social thinking".

There is a sense in which his subsequent political career has been a kind of Calvary, so that he finished up in 1977 virtually isolated as the lone Dail representative of the Socialist Labour Party.

His stubborn insistence on seeing Ireland as it was rather than through the customary Ah-sure-it's-going-to-be-all-right blinkers put him outside the pale of the cosy rituals of party politics or what he called "the conspiracy of agreed lies".

Such was the capacity for delusion in the 1940s that when Liam O'Leary made a film documentary for the Clann na Poblachta party showing poverty and squalor in Dublin he was accused of staging it.

"The reality of mass unemployment and emigration was in complete conflict with the speeches Dev made about the Irish language and Partition being the two great problems we were facing," Browne claimed.

It was this idea of a man with the courage to face facts however unflattering that appealed to Ballagh as a subject for painting: coming to terms with unpalatable realities was as much the function of art as of politics.

"But looking at a lot of Irish art you'd think it happened completely independently of the social matrix. What passed for true Irishness in art was a kind of romantic thing called the poetic genre." Looking at such paintings, as someone once remarked, was like looking through mists of colour.

"Artists, like politicians in the 1950s, were turning their backs on social reality to create a kind of mythical world of landscape which never existed."

This sort of romanticised rural idyll had not been part of Ballagh's experience growing up in the city. It had always seemed dishonest for him to attempt to paint in such a way. But by placing Browne in the Connemara setting he could now deal in art terms with a lot of issues and themes he'd difficulty in addressing as an urban artist. "Landscape has been such a significant part of Irish art yet it is something that living in the city I've always felt unable to deal with adequately."

Connemara was Browne's idea. He'd gone there first after becoming a Minister in 1948, feeling it would be hypocritical not to learn Irish.

"My friends can't stand the poverty of it all. The barrenness. The endless walls. The sense of the suffering people must have gone through to survive and of the suffering of those who had to get out."

All of which is implicit in the cold clear lighting of the portrait. This is not a Connemara man seen through the usual purple mists.

The stones Browne stands on are so real that some actually spill out onto the floor; a *trompe l'oeil* effect so convincing that it's hard to distinguish them from their painted counterparts.

"My parents came from the West, emigrants like tens of thousands of others." They both died of tuberculosis when Browne was a child. He survived to become the doctor who led the campaign for its successful eradication.

So in a sense he has come back to his roots. But without any sentimental illusions. Meet him in Dublin and he is apt to be wearing a *crios* around his waist. Ballagh shows him in an Aran sweater. But that's as far as that kind of "Irishness" goes. That is part of the irony of the portrait.

Nobody commissioned Ballagh to paint Browne: it was his own choice. Newspaper tycoon Gerry McGuinness had been giving out on the Mike Murphy radio show about whiners and begrudgers, claiming that the real patriots in contemporary Ireland were the Ben Dunnes and Michael Smurfits. These were the men to whom statues ought to be erected. Ballagh decided that rather than celebrate people like that who had made a lot of money for themselves ("not that they should necessarily be faulted for that") he'd paint a man who always acted with integrity and not self-interest: this would be his patriot.

He hadn't met Browne before although he had joined him in a protest march ("pushing Rachel in a pram") when Bernadette Devlin had been arrested in 1968. But he identified with his unsentimental and unwavering commitment to socialism.

Two of the books shown at Browne's feet — to prevent even the most casual observer mistaking him for a Connemara fisherman — are by Marx and Beckett, not the average Irish politician's preferred reading. The Gaelic title of the third book, *Fód a bháile,* which carries on the spine the enbossed signature 'Riobard Ballagh', is a fisherman's traditional expression for coming ashore.

"There are all sorts of political connotations to the use of Irish in Dublin. But when I was with Browne in Connemara it seemed perfectly natural that he should speak to his neighbours in Irish. It was a reminder that for all the abuse surrounding it, it is still a significant part of our cultural heritage."

The picture, which was first exhibited at Edinburgh Festival in 1985, is as much a portrait of Ballagh as of Browne. It merges the form and content of the portrait series with that of the autobiographical series. Through it he finally resolves the recurring questions of cultural identity and Irishness. He has arrived at an enduring ikon of his time and place.

POSTSCRIPT

The confrontation of opposites has been a recurring pattern in all Robert Ballagh's art: modernism versus tradition, fine art versus popular art, hand-made versus mechanical, urban reality versus rural idyll, Irishness versus international conformity. Both in form and in content his painting reveals the dialectic of his own development as an artist in society.

The apparent contradictions are in fact logical turning points in a continuing journey of self-discovery as he gradually moves from the general to the particular — from an idea of art to an idea of his own personal art — and then out again from the particular to the general to arrive at a universal vision, responding honestly, as James Joyce did, to his own experience.

Within the terms of each phase he has gone through there has always developed the possibility of a new phase. Each seemingly fortuitous change in direction has been locked into what went before.

To say that his art is the consequence of a complex social process rather than of a flash of genius is not to diminish it or to reduce it to the mundane, any more than to describe life in terms of the evolution of the species is to deny man his unique quality.

To appreciate the intricate interaction of personal experience and the social and economic conditions of which art is often a consequence is to appreciate the magic and beauty of his painting.

Pop art pushed Ballagh into the limelight as a painter when he was still virtually a beginner. He had to do his learning in public. He was already an established artist before he began to find out what kind of artist it was really in his nature to be. This had the effect of making him unusually responsive to his own immediate experience. There is a sense of look-what-I-have-discovered-now freshness and enthusiasm about most of his work.

His lack of formal training meant that, like many of the rock musicians and the great jazz players, he started out by familiarising himself with certain effects he needed rather than with the whole repertoire of painting: he developed whatever techniques were suitable for expressing his particular choice of subjects. His paintings were a reflection of his own ideas about painting instead of a response to established art college ways of seeing things. This can have the disadvantage of leaving an artist overly dependent on technique. Vision is constrained by a narrowness of range. The result is sometimes a certain tightness in the painting.

Ballagh is well aware of this. "Keep it loose, Bobby", Micheal Farrell is still inclined to tease him. But much of the tightness in his painting is by now more apparent than real. He is moving ever closer to the realism of Vermeer, in whose work details that seem very carefully modelled turn out on closer scrutiny to be little more than the touch of a brush.

"I think a painter has to work real tight and accurate first in order to understand the whole thing. If you're going to use shorthand for the depiction of any sort of reality, you've got to have the longhand first. Barnett Newman took forty years to build up to the gesture of painting a stripe down a canvas. It seemed easy but it wasn't."

The smallness and social cohesiveness of Dublin, with its inextricable overlapping of the provincial and the cosmopolitan, the traditional and the modern, a city in which different walks of life — intellectual, artistic, business, professional, administrative, political, educational, religious — could mingle with first-name familiarity, made it unlikely that Ballagh would share the sense of alienation and separateness cultivated by his Modernist peers in the larger capitals of London, Paris or New York.

As a child of popular culture — comics, movies, rock music — he was in any way at odds with the inherent elitism of international art. It was more natural for him to regard painting as a means to communicate with the many rather than the few. He instinctively distrusted the tyranny of the cult of the unique art object. In this he turned out to be in tune with the shift in western philosophical thought away from a unified system of logic — typified by Jacques Derrida's attempt to "deconstruct" the logical categories of philosophy and science in order (as the young Irish philosopher Richard Kearney put it) "to rediscover the infinitely differentiating richness of language". Ballagh was to show in painting what Joyce had shown in literature: that truth is not *one* but *many.*

He grew up within a few streets of the house on Sandymount Avenue where the poet W.B. Yeats was born. He used play on a Sandymount Strand immortalised by James Joyce. Among his neighbours were the playwright Brendan Behan in Anglesea Road and the poet Patrick Kavanagh on Pembroke Road. The experience of maturing in a city so richly pervaded by literary awareness inevitably prompted him to question the dogmatic Modernist adherence to a purely formal art which denied this any relevance.

Not that art for art's sake didn't have its appeal in Dublin in the 1970s. There was a growing sense of impotence in face of the failure of politics in the North. The mood was not unlike that in the Vienna of Freud and Schnitzler at the turn of the century when power switched drastically from the enlightened liberal bourgeoisie to the mass movements of anti-Semitism, socialism and nationalism (vividly described by Carl E. Schorske in his book *Fin-de-Siecle Vienna:* "The life of art became a substitute for the life of action. Indeed, as civic action proved increasingly futile, art became almost a religion, the source of meaning and the food for the soul").

But Ballagh, while he shared the general sense of helplessness, was to confront rather than retreat from the unpalatable reality. Unravelling the whole complicated nature of Irish identity which was at its root — the pluralism of cultures and traditions — became the preoccupation of his art.

He has emerged as a painter in an Ireland particularly susceptible to his creative vision. In a sense that vision is also a response to the circumstances of the society within which he finds himself.

"The artist can only be of his own time," he says. "He has to play with the cards he's dealt."

Ballagh photograph of a Dublin doorway illustrating a special limited edition of Joyce's *Dubliners* published in New York, 1986.

INDEX

(Page numbers in bold indicate illustrations)

M

MacDermott, Philip, 141, 158, 172
MacGonigal, Maurice, 162
Maclise, Daniel, 124
Magritte, Rene, 110-112
Mahaffy, Professor, 42
Mahon, Derek, 196
Malone Dies, 196
Malone, James, 12
Man and Socialism in Cuba, 76
Manley, Michael, 100
Manne-Brähammer, Marianne, 190
Manzoni, Piero, 167
Marcus, David, 141
Marcuse, Herbert, 76, 183
Marquez, Gabriel Garcia, 183
Martin, Davey, 54
Marx, Karl, 12, 76, 158, 200
Matisse, Henri, 113
McAvock, Desmond, 166
McGovern, Barry, 13, 196, **197**
McGuinness, Gerry, 200
McGuinness, Norah, 27, 81, 102
McGrath, Father, 167
McKiernan, Dr Eoin, 151
McLoughlin, Dr T.A., 101
McLaverty, Michael, 163
McNabb, Theo, 132
McNamara, Billy, 39
McQuaid, Dr John Charles, 42
Meninas, Las, 151, 154
Merediths, Miss, 38
Michelangelo, Buonarroti, 140
Mies van der Rohe, 52
Milners, George, 60, 181, 192
Mural art, 14
Modernism, 12, 14-16, 27, 52-53, 65,
71-72, 75, 108, 113, 119, 123, 127, 130,
138, 141-42, 158, 161, 167-68, 176, 201
Molloy, 196

Monroe, Marilyn, 118, 167
Morellet, Francois, 100
Mosse, Paul, 72
Motherwell, Robert, 109
Mr and Mrs Andrews, 26-27, 87
Mulcahy, John, 99
Muldoon, Paul, 13, 28
Murphy, Bill, 127
Murphy, Mike, 200
Murphy, Ned, 29
Museum of Drawers, 167
Museum of Modern Art, 96, 106
Muybridge, Edward, 165

N

Newman, Barnett, 12, 71, 108, 202
Noland, Kenneth, 167
North, violence in, 13, 27-28, 57, 75,
77, 81-82, 84, 90-92, 100, 104, 124, 127,
135-36, 165-66, 203

O

Ó Briain, Colm, 20, 133-134, 196
O'Brien, Anthony, 72
O'Brien, Conor Cruise, 76-79
O'Brien, Flann, 137-38
O'Casey, Sean, 101
Ósiobhain, Blaithin, 109
O'Connell, Eilis, 179
O'Connor, Francis, 104
O'Doherty, Brian, 104
O'Doherty, Fr E.F., 20
Ó hUadhaigh, Robert, 194
Oils, 108, 116, 118
Oldenberg, Claes, 167
O'Leary, Liam, 199
Olympia Theatre, 25, 43, 142
Op art, 14

Y

Robert Ballagh speaking on behalf of the visual artists at the inaugural meeting of Aosdána, the affiliation of 150 creative people who have "established a reputation for achievement and distinction in ther discipline." The Taoiseach, Dr Garret FitzGerald, and the Fianna Fail leader, Charles Haughey, were invited guests.

From the outside looking in at Ballagh's retrospective in the Municipal Gallery of Lund, Sweden, in early 1983.

LIST OF WORKS

Measurements are given in inches, height before width. In some cases it has not been possible to trace the present owners. This listing does not include drawings, prints, designs or photographs.

1967

Torso. Metal construction, 24 x 18. Destroyed.
Pinball. Metal construction, 24 x 18. Destroyed.
Matchbox. Acrylic on canvas, 66 x 40. Collection of artist.
Blade. Acrylic on canvas, 72 x 36. Arts Council.
Ice Cream. Acrylic on canvas, 60 x 53. John Maguire, Dublin.

1968

Brillo Box. Acrylic on canvas, 60 x 60. Destroyed.
Diamond No. 1. Acrylic on canvas, 48 x 48. Trust Houses Forte Ltd.
Diamond No. 2. Acrylic on canvas, 48 x 48. Arts Council of Ireland.
Diamond No. 3. Acrylic on canvas, 48 x 48. Bank of Ireland.
Map Series No. 1. Acrylic on canvas, 48 x 48.
Map Series No. 2. Acrylic on canvas, 48 x 48.

Map Series No. 3. Acrylic on canvas, 48 x 48. Collection of artist.

1969

Map murals commissioned by Fitzwilton Ltd. Acrylic on canvas. Three murals, 84 x 196 each, Trinity College, Dublin.
Marchers. Acrylic on 4 canvasses, 72 x 72. Bank of Ireland.
Marchers. Acrylic on 5 canvasses, 60 x 60. Mr. & Mrs. E.J. Neville, Dublin.
Marchers. Acrylic and silkscreen on plywood, 48 x 36. Collection of artist.
Marchers. Acrylic on canvas, 66 x 36. Trinity College, Dublin.
Marchers. Vacuum formed plastic, 50 x 50. Collection of artist.
Marchers. Silkscreen and acrylic on plywood, 48 x 37. Coras Trachtala/ Irish Export Board.
Marchers. Silkscreen and acrylic on plywood, 34 x 30. Alan Diskin, Dublin.
Marchers. Acrylic and screenprinting on canvas, 50 x 50. Collection of artist.

Marchers. Silkscreen and acrylic on canvas, 48 x 43. Hugh Lane Municipal Gallery, Dublin.
Burning Monk. Acrylic on 3 canvasses, 24 x 72. Tony Hickey, London.
Firing Squad. Acrylic on canvas, 66 x 54. Collection of artist.
Firing Squad 2. Acrylic on canvas, 50 x 70. Collection of artist.
Refugees. Acrylic on canvas, 20 x 20. Collection of artist.

1969-1970

The Rape of the Sabines after David. Acrylic on canvas, 72 x 96. Crawford Municipal Gallery, Cork.
Liberty at the Barricades after Delacroix. Acrylic on canvas, 72 x 96. Bank of Ireland.
The Third of May after Goya. Acrylic on canvas, 72 x 96. Hugh Lane Municipal Gallery, Dublin.

1970

Homage to David. Acrylic on canvas, 60 x 48. Gordon Lambert, Dublin.
The Turkish Bath after Ingres. Acrylic on canvas, 72 x 72. Mr. & Mrs. Finghin O'Driscoll, Monaghan.

1970-1971

Dolly Mixtures. Acrylic on canvas, 60 x 60. Stephen Pearce, Cork.
Gob stoppers. Acrylic on canvas, 56 x 56, Gulf Oil Corporation, Pittsburg, United States.
Liquorice Comfits 1. Acrylic on canvas, 26 x 26. Ruth Durley, Dublin.
Liquorice Comfits 2. Acrylic on canvas, 56 x 56. Destroyed.
Liquorice Comfits 3. Acrylic on canvas, 62 x 40. Private Collection, Dublin.
Liquorice Allsorts. Acrylic on canvas, 44 x 72. Destroyed.
Iced Caramels. Acrylic on canvas, 40 x 56. Hugh Lane Municipal Gallery, Dublin.
Chocolate Beans. Acrylic on canvas, 30 x 56. Christian Medical College, Vellore, India.
Liquorice Allsorts 1. Acrylic on canvas, 60 x 36. Cecil King, Dublin.
Seven Cakes. Acrylic on canvas, 54 x 54. Collection of artist.
Three Cakes. Acrylic on canvas, 60 x 36. Destroyed.
Two Cakes. Acrylic on canvas, 60 x 60. Collection of artist.
One cake. Acrylic on canvas, 18 x 18. Collection of artist.
Ducks. Acrylic on canvas, 42 diameter. The late Sir Basil Goulding, Dublin.
Deer and Faun. Acrylic on canvas, 42 diameter. Destroyed.
Stag. Acrylic on canvas, 52 x 38. Destroyed.
Faun. Acrylic on canvas, 20 diameter. Mr. & Mrs. E.J. Neville, Dublin.

1971

James Connolly. Acrylic on canvas, 60 x 40. Sam Stephenson, Dublin.
Mural for ESB. Acrylic on canvas, 84 x 204. ESB, Dublin.
Portrait of Gordon Lambert. Acrylic and silkscreen on canvas, 72 x 36. Gordon Lambert, Dublin.

1972

Portrait of David Hendriks. Acrylic and silkscreen on canvas, 72 x 36. David Hendriks, Dublin.
Three People with a Jackson Pollock. Acrylic on canvas, 96 x 144. Trinity College, Dublin.
Three People with a Robert Ballagh. Acrylic on canvas, 96 x 96. Bank of Ireland.
Girl with a Barnett Newman. Acrylic on canvas, 96 x 72. Bank of Ireland.
Man with a Cecil King. Acrylic on canvas, 96 x 48. Bank of Ireland.
Woman with a Guiseppe Capogrossi. Acrylic on canvas, 96 x 48. Bank of Ireland.

Woman with a Pierre Soulages. Acrylic on canvas, 96 x 48. Bank of Ireland.
Two People with an Adolf Gotleib. Acrylic on canvas, 96 x 48. Bank of Ireland.
Man with a Lucio Fontana. Acrylic on canvas, 84 x 28. Gordon Lambert, Dublin.
Man with a Piet Mondrian. Acrylic on canvas, 96 x 48. Louisiana Museum, Denmark.
Girl and a Mark Rothko. Acrylic on canvas, 96 x 48. Mr. & Mrs. Michael Costello, Dublin.
Two People with a Jackson Pollock. Acrylic on canvas, 96 x 96. Private Collection, France.
Two People with a Robert Indiana. Acrylic on canvas, 96 x 96. Private collection, France.

1973

Man with a Frank Stella. Acrylic on canvas, 96 x 96. Bank of Ireland.
Two Men and a Roy Lichtenstein. Acrylic on canvas, 96 x 96. P.J. Carroll & Co., Dundalk.
Child with an Andy Warhol. Acrylic on canvas, 72 x 48. Galerie Isy Brachot, Brussels.
Man with a Rene Magritte. Acrylic on canvas, 92 x 48. Private collection, Belgium.
Man and a Morris Louis. Acrylic on canvas, 40 x 32. Private collection, Belgium.
Child with an Andy Warhol. Acrylic on canvas, 32 x 40. Private collection, Switzerland.
Two People with an Elsworth Kelly. Acrylic on canvas, 32 x 40. Private collection, Switzerland.
Couple with a Clifford Still. Acrylic on canvas, 92 x 92. Private collection, Milan, Italy.
Boy and Girl with a Roy Lichtenstein. Acrylic on canvas, 96 x 72. Private collection, Belgium.

Woman and Jackson Pollock. Acrylic on canvas, 96 x 72. Private Collection, Brussels.
Winchester 73. Oil on canvas, 12 x 12. Collection of artist.

1973-1975

Portrait in Green, Hans Hoffman. Oil on canvas. Mr. & Mrs. Paul Daly, Tipperary.
Blue Mona Lisa. Oil on canvas, 38 x 21. Collection of artist.
Silver Painting, Andy Warhol. Oil on canvas. Private Collection, Dublin.
St. Patrick. Oil on canvas. Hal Maloney, Sedona, Arizona.
Rachel/Marilyn. Oil on canvas. Fr. McGrath, Tipperary.
Portraits of James Joyce, Sean O'Casey, G.B. Shaw, Oscar Wilde, Brendan Behan. Acrylic on canvas, 3 x 3 each. Aer Lingus.

1974

Man with an Adolf Gotleib. Acrylic on canvas, 92 x 92. Collection of artist.
People with a Frank Stella. Acrylic on canvas, 96 x 48. Private collection, Switzerland.
Woman and a Ferdinand Leger. Acrylic on canvas, 72 x 48. Private collection, Brussels.
Woman and a Francis Bacon. Acrylic on canvas, 96 x 72. Private collection, Brussels.
Woman and a Victor Vasarely. Acrylic on canvas, 96 x 48. Private collection, Brussels.
Woman and a Jasper Johns. Acrylic on canvas, 96 x 48. Private collection, Brussels.
Man and a Rene Magritte. Acrylic on canvas, 96 x 48. Private collection, Brussels.
Girl and a Pablo Picasso. Acrylic on canvas, 96 x 48. Private collection, Brussels.
Man and a Piet Mondrian. Acrylic on

canvas, 32 x 16. Private collection, Belgium.

Man and a Tom Wesselman. Acrylic on canvas, 32 x 16. Private collection, Brussels.

Woman and a Kuni Sugari. Acrylic on canvas, 32 x 16. Private collection. Brussels.

Man with a Frank Stella. Acrylic on canvas, 32 x 16. Private collection, Belgium.

Two Children and a Roy Lichtenstein. Acrylic on canvas, 96 x 48. Private collection, Brussels.

Woman and a Ferdinand Leger. Acrylic on canvas, 24 x 18. Private collection, Brussels.

Figures and a Michelangelo Pistoletto. Acrylic on canvas milk plastic mirror, 96 x 72. Collection of artist.

Man and a Rene Magritte with Cut-out Standing Boy. Acrylic on canvas, life size. Mr. & Mrs. Alvin Cutler, United States.

Cut-out with a Robert Morris. Acrylic on canvas, life size. Collection of artist.

Cut-out with a Josef Albers. Acrylic on canvas, life size. Crawford Municipal Gallery, Cork.

Cut-out with an Alexander Calder. Acrylic on canvas with painted construction, life size. The late Sir Basil Goulding.

Cut out with a Dan Flavin. Acrylic on canvas with neon construction, life size. Ulster Museum, Belfast.

Cut-out with a Piet Mondrian. Acrylic on canvas, life size. Collection of artist.

Cut-out with a David Smith. Acrylic on canvas, life size. Collection of aritst.

Cut-out with a Roy Lichtenstein. Acrylic on canvas, life size. Conal O'Sullivan, London.

Cut-out with a Bridget Riley. Acrylic on canvas, life size. Collection of artist.

Cut-out with a Kumi Sugai. Acrylic on canvas, life size. The late Sir Basil Goulding.

1975

People and a Leger. Acrylic and oil on canvas, 62 x 50. Private collection, Switzerland.

Two Men and a Picasso. Acrylic and oil on canvas, 30 x 30. Private collection, Paris.

People and a Matisse. Acrylic and oil on canvas, 51 x 32. Galerie Lilliane Francois, Paris.

Two People with a Robert Indiana. Acrylic and oil on canvas. Private collection, Switzerland.

Three People with a Morris Louis. Acrylic and oil on canvas, 96 x 60. Private collection, Belgium.

Man and a Tom Wesselman. Acrylic and oil on canvas. Collection of artist.

Two Men and a Robert Ballagh. Acrylic and oil on canvas, 42 x 24. Mr. and Mrs. Patrick Walshe.

Portrait of the late M. Smadja. Acrylic and oil on canvas. Collection of artist.

People and a modern painting. Plastic laminate, 120 x 912. Quinnsworth Ltd.

Laurence Sterne (study). Oil and acrylic on canvas, 72 x 24. Elizabeth Ballagh, Dublin.

The Life and Opinions of Tristram Shandy, Gentleman (study). Oil and acrylic on canvas, 25 x 180. Mr. & Mrs. George McClelland, Dublin.

Portrait of Laurence Sterne. Oil and acrylic on canvas, 58 x 144. Quinnsworth Ltd.

The Life and Opinions of T. Shandy, Gentleman. Oil and acrylic on canvas, 60 x 432. Quinnsworth Ltd.

1976

Joseph Sheridan le Fanu. Oil and acrylic on canvas, 60 x 48. Arts Council, Dublin.

The Art Lover. Acrylic and oil on canvas, 30 x 24. Desmond and Margaret Downes, Dublin.

Screen for Gordon Lambert. Four

canvas panels, painted both sides, 60 x 18 each. Gordon Lambert, Dublin.

Studio with Modigliani print. Oil and acrylic on canvas, 24 x 24. Liam Kelly, Belfast.

My Studio, 1969. Oil and acrylic on canvas, 96 x 72. Collection of artist.

My Studio, 1969 (study). Oil and acrylic on canvas, 24 x 36. Brian McSwiney, Dublin.

1977

The Barracks (from the series "The Third Policeman"). Mixed media, 42 x 42. Richard Wood, Cork.

Ceel Window (from "The Third Policeman"). Mixed media, 30 x 24. Noel Pearson, Dublin.

Room (from "The Third Policeman"). Acrylic and oil on canvas, 30 x 24. Mr. & Mrs. John Gore-Grimes, Dublin.

Day and Night (from "The Third Policeman"). Acrylic and oil on canvas, 30 x 24. Mr. & Mrs. John Gore-Grimes, Dublin.

The Atomic Theory (from "The Third Policeman"). Acrylic and oil on canvas, 30 x 24. Mr. & Mrs. Robin Walker, Dublin.

Mathers (from "The Third Policeman"). Mixed media, 30 x 24. Mr. & Mrs. Paul Daly, Tipperary.

Oh, Mona. Oil and acrylic on canvas, 38 x 24. House of Humour and satire, Gabravo, Bulgaria.

People and a Kenneth Noland and Ellsworth Kelly. Mixed media, 2 x 2. Museum of Drawers, Bern, Switzerland.

No. 3. Oil and acrylic on canvas, 72 x 96. Hugh Lane Municipal Gallery, Dublin.

The Conversation. Acrylic and oil on canvas, 72 x 96. Colin Haddick, Northern Ireland.

Kite for Kilkenny (study). Mixed media. Butler House, Kilkenny.

Kite for Kilkenny. Mixed media. Collection of artist.

Portrait of Walter Curley, former US Ambassador, and Mrs. Curley. Mixed media.

1978

Dawn at Platin. Acrylic and oil on canvas, 36 x 24. Minister of Transport and Power, Dublin.

Portrait of James Plunkett. Acrylic and oil on canvas, 60 x 48. Philip MacDermott, Dublin.

Portrait of Brendan Smith. Oil on canvas, 60 x 60. Olympia Theatre, Dublin.

1979

Portrait of Bernadette Greevy. Oil on canvas, 48 x 48. Gordon Lambert, Dublin.

Bernadette Greevy and family. Oil on canvas, 24 x 18. Bernadette Greevy, Dublin.

Portrait of Hugh Leonard. Oil on canvas, 48 x 60. Hugh Leonard, Dublin.

Oh, Not Again. Oil and acrylic on canvas, 24 x 36. House of Humour and Satire, Gabravo, Bulgaria.

Inside No. 3. Oil and acrylic on canvas, 72 x 72. Ulster Museum, Belfast.

No. 53, Winter in Ronda. Acrylic and oil on canvas, 72 x 96. Central Bank of Ireland, Dublin.

Oh, Not Again. Oil and acrylic on canvas, 24 x 36. House of Humour and Satire, Bulgaria.

The Distant Past. Oil and acrylic on canvas, painting for book cover, 30 x 29. Mr. & Mrs. Stephen O'Mara, Dublin.

Call My Brother Back. Oil and acrylic on canvas, painting for book cover, 30 x 29. Mr. & Mrs. Philip MacDermott, Dublin.

Body and Soul. Oil and acrylic on canvas, painting for book cover, 16 x 12. Mr. & Mrs. Philip MacDermott, Dublin.

A Life of Her Own. Oil and acrylic on canvas, painting for book cover, 24 x 26. Beaufield Mews, Dublin.
Jack Lynch. Oil and acrylic on canvas, painting for magazine cover, 28 x 22. Collection of artist.

1980

Portrait of Michael Scott. Oil on canvas, 36 x 36. Michael Scott, Dublin.
The Decade of Endeavour, Portrait of C.J. Haughey. Oil on canvas, 60 x 48. C.J. Haughey, Dublin.
Dubin Theatre Festival. Oil and acrylic on canvas, painting for poster, 24 x 18. Micael Colgan, Dublin.

1981

The Downes Family at Knockatillane. Oil on canvas, 48 x 60. Mr. & Mrs. Desmond Downes, Dublin.
Page from an Irish Manuscript. Acrylic and oil on canvas, 24 x 18. House of Humour and Satire, Bulgaria.
The Mallin Family, Oil on canvas, 48 x 48. Mr. & Mrs. Michael Mallin. Its Handy When People Don't Die. Oil on canvas, painting for book cover, 24 x 36. Philip MacDermott.
Is This Thy Day. Oil and acrylic on canvas, painting for book cover, 12 x 8, Philip MacDermott.
Black and White. Oil on canvas, painting for book cover, 18 x 12. Philip MacDermott.

1982

Inside No. 3, After Modernisation. Acrylic and oil on canvas, 84 x 60. Collection of artist.
Upstairs No. 3. Acrylic and oil on canvas, 72 x 96. Collection of artist.
Gay Byrne (commissioned by Irish Biscuits Ltd). Oil on canvas, 16 x 16. Mr. and Mrs. Gay Byrne.
The Three Brothers. Oil and acrylic on canvas, painting for book cover, 8 x 12.

Philip MacDermott.
Eamon de Valera. Oil on canvas, painting for postage stamp, 12 x 8. Dept. of Post & Telegraphs.

1983

Andrew Jackson. Oil on canvas, painting for postage stamp, 12 x 8. Dept. of Post & Telegraphs.
Sean MacDiarmada. Oil on canvas, painting for postage stamp, 12 x 8. Dept. of Post & Telegraphs.
94 St. Stephen's Green. Oil on canvas, 48 x 36. Smurfit Bank Ltd.
World Communications Year 1. Acrylic on canvas, painting for postage stamp, 12 x 8. Dept. of Post & Telegraphs.
World Communications Year II. Acrylic on canvas, painting for postage stamp, 12 x 8. Dept. of Post & Telegraphs.

1984

Highfield (originally titled The Pause That Refreshes). Oil on canvas, 73 x 54. COllection of artist.
Portrait of District Justice Ó hUadhaigh. Oil on canvas, 42 x 30. Commissioned by the Association of Criminal Lawyers.
I See Red. Self-portrait. Oil on canvas, 12 x 8. Collection of Vincent Ferguson.
Man Drawing a Recumbent Woman. Oil on canvas, 48 x 24. Collection Albrecht Durer Haus, Nurmberg.
Peace. Poster design. Oil on canvas, 30 x 30. Collection Union of Artists, USSR.

1985

Dr Noel Browne. Oil on canvas, 72 x 54. Collection of artist.
Lost Innocence. Book cover. Oil on canvas, 18 x 24. Collection Barry O'Halloran.
Dunsink Observatory. Stamp design. Oil on canvas, 12 x 8. Collection An Post.

First Flight by an Irishman. Stamp design. Oil on canvas, 12 x 8. Collection An Post.

Thomas Ashe. Stamp design. Oil on canvas, 12 x 8. Collection An Post.

1986

Aer Lingus. Stamp design. Oil on canvas, 12 x 8. Collection An Post.

Barry McGuigan. Oil on canvas, 18 x 12. Collection Irish Independent.

The Advertising Book. Book cover design. Oil on canvas.

The Fastnet Lighthouse. Stamp design. Oil on canvas, 12 x 8. Collection An Post.

The Kish Lighthouse. Stamp design. Oil on canvas, 12 x 8. Collection An Post.

Innovation. Oil on canvas, 16 x20. Collection Cara Computors.

The School Show. Oil on canvas, 30 x 20. Collection The Arts Council.

A miniature of Betty, painted as a birthday present.